Aliens in Celtic History and Legends: Cases from Britain

ISBN-13: 978-1478356387
ISBN-10: 1478356383

Medieval Welsh literature is filled with references to non-human peoples who have visited Britain. There are the people of Annwfn, the 'Eingl' (angels), the Coranieid and the family of Llwyd Cil Coed. Some were friendly and some were hostile but all interacted with the Britons in history and legend.

At the same time there are certain reoccurring motifs which can be best explained by reference to modern science and technology. There are marvellous bottles which can keep milk fresh and liquid warm all day, hypnotic music which sends people to sleep, strange sounds of thunder which precede the arrival of non-human characters, and a singular floating glass fortress which forms the entrance to Annwfn, a subterranean world only spoken of in legend. This book critically examines medieval Welsh literature to answer the questions: Could some of our history and legends have been inspired by contact with alien races? And, if so, how probable is it?

Melissa Westwind is an academic from the UK. She holds degrees in medieval British language and literature and lives in a university city in Britain. She wishes to break the silence regarding the possibility that the history and legends of the Celtic languages may preserve traces of contact with extraterrestrial species.

Prologue

The most extraordinary case of illness transmitted from animals to man [in medieval Irish] is that described in the Annals of Connacht in 1224.

A heavy and terrible shower fell in part of Connacht this year, that is in Tir Maine and in Sodain and in Ui Diarmata and in Clann Taidc, which brought about disease and very great sickness among the cows and beasts of those regions after they had eaten grass and leaves and when men drank of the milk of these cattle and ate of their flesh, they suffered internal pains and various diseases.

This description strangely prefigures the contamination of pasture and hence meat and milk by rain-borne radioactive fall-out, as happened in many parts of Europe after the explosion at the Chernobyl nuclear plant in 1986. I have not been able to find any explanation of the 1224 episode. (Fergus Kelly, Early Irish Farming, 1998, p.195)

This is how Fergus Kelly describes the events recorded in the Irish Annals of Connacht for 1224, the year of the death of the king of Connacht, Cathal Crobhdearg Ua Conchobair. Kelly's scholarly confusion is what, in part, inspired the book you are reading today. He is a senior professor at Dublin Institute for Advanced Studies and one of the greatest authorities ever to write on Old and Middle Irish. If *he* allows himself to express some bewilderment and even hint at something beyond the normal, surely other interested parties, with no academic reputation on the line and nothing to lose by being wrong might be permitted to engage in some speculation of their own.

The main part of this book will be spent examining other hard-to-explain events occurring in medieval Britain. However, the meticulous reader may have already noticed that this book is not confined to commenting on historic events. In medieval times the line between fact and fiction is not always very clear and factual accounts often give fantastic stories, whilst fantastic anecdotes often have some element of truth to them. This book will therefore also examine a few fairytale motifs and reoccurring items which acquire an uncanny significance in the light of modern UFO accounts, and other, stranger stories in older languages.

This book is not intended to be an academic thesis. Although I will introduce each case-file in its academic context, complete with examination of both primary text and secondary commentaries, when it comes to my own interpretation I will be speculating quite heavily. The texts we will be reading cover some of the strangest events and hardest to explain stories found across five hundred years of the literature and therefore "normal" explanations are unlikely to fit very well (although they will be considered). Readers interested primarily or only in the facts can confine themselves to the "Introduction" and the "Text" part of each "Case". Likewise, readers interested in only the conclusions (the possible contact that medieval people had with aliens) and not especially interested in medieval texts or my methods of translating them are invited to confine themselves primarily to the "Interpretation" part of each case. After presenting all of the cases I will evaluate how safe my interpretations are, and finish by restating my strongest conclusions.

Having said that, readers need make only the following allowances whilst reading – that aliens may exist, may have visited Britain, and may have formed the basis of history and legends in the past. Although my "Interpretation" sections are deliberately speculative, they speculate based only on the facts which have already been established, they do not twist facts to suit them. In the introduction to every case I offer the key editions and translations by which people may check my translations (which are used throughout the text).

It is often argued that extraordinary claims require extraordinary evidence. However, in medieval Welsh literature the idea that races of non-human intelligent life-forms inhabited the Earth was not extraordinary, but rather commonly believed. Generally the idea of life on other planets was not even considered, but before the Scientific Revolution and before the world had been fully explored many strange things were believed to be true. I must leave it up to my readers to decide whether any of my case-files have their origins in accounts of contact with non-human life-forms. I only contend that they may have been considered to do so by medieval writers and their audiences.

Contents

Introduction

The chances of anything coming from Mars...

The chance that you will ever encounter an intelligent member of an extra-terrestrial species is astronomically low. Realistically, of the 74 exoplanets confirmed by Kepler to be in the habitable zone in our galaxy[1] , none are likely to have undergone the very rare circumstances which lead to complex life. In addition, based on current knowledge of theoretical technology, even if we managed to harness clean nuclear pulse or fission power it would still take 400 (earth) years to reach the media's favourite 'close neighbour', Gliese 581. At present only the earth's longest-lived trees, sponges and corals would be able to survive a trip that long, and aliens would unlikely be impressed by that kind of visitor[2]. Thinking evolutionarily, the chances of a reflective, inquisitive and technological species developing, not to mention one that is also motivated to explore space, seems very low. Finally, considering the lessons of history, any contact with other civilisations with (necessarily, for them to reach us) superior technology would be unlikely to end amicably.

Considering all of these things, we are left with the miniscule although not-quite-zero percent chance that intelligent aliens will visit each year. Even if you lived to be 100, you would hardly affect your odds of seeing them. This has led to the majority of "realistic" space drama being set in the uncertain future, where humans are exploring space themselves. Unfortunately based on current knowledge of physics, space travel, and even looking into the future appears to be impossible. This of course relegates future sightings to the realm of science fiction.

There are still a few other ways in which we might be able to encounter extraterrestrial creatures, albeit indirectly. Looking backwards, the earth is around 4.5 billion years old. At present estimate, the age of the galaxy

---

[1] As of June 2012, although there are over 1,000 more candidates waiting to be confirmed.

[2] Our best current bet for significantly longer lives may be the *2045 Avatar* project which aims to bring immortality to the human mind by uploading it into a computer and giving it a holographic (robotic in the short term) body by the year 2045 (see: www.2045.com).

is around three times that, and some planets developed very much earlier in its history. Very roughly, we know that the Earth is developing a civilisation with space technology for the first time right now, that is, after 4.5 billion years of its history[3]. We also know that there was twice that amount of time *before* the Earth was created for the oldest planets in the galaxy to develop their own civilisations with similar technology before the Earth was even formed. Therefore any potential alien civilisation is just as likely to have visited in any given year in the Earth's history, as to visit in this year. This is the real advantage of looking to the past. Because of the massive number of years the Earth has been available for alien visitation, the chances that aliens of some form could have visited one year in the planet's past are 45 million times greater than the chance that they will have visited one year during your life if you live to be 100 years old. That's worth saying twice: statistically aliens are far, far more likely to have visited in the past, than they are to have visited in the last hundred years.

This logic is very simplistic of course. If extra-terrestrial civilisations don't go extinct, the number of intelligent species with space-technology present in the galaxy is likely to increase over time, especially if they contact each other and can accelerate technological advancement. If more species with space-technology are exploring the galaxy, there is a greater likelihood that we will be visited. Human activities on the planet earth, particularly the use of radio signals and the sending of probes like *Voyager 1* might also encourage visitors. Overall we may be more likely to be visited this year than in previous years, simply because we may be more interesting and valuable to potential contactors. Furthermore, for most of the history of the Earth as we know it, there has not been any record-keeping intelligent life-form present, and therefore we could only know about the visits of aliens if they left some sort of message behind. Many of the worlds more impressive monuments, like the pyramids of Mesoamerica and Egypt, or the Nazca lines, the architecture of Tiwanaku, and various astronomically-aligned monuments in Europe and Asia have been attributed to aliens, with generally little mainstream acceptance.

---

[3] *Voyager 1* is currently the only man-made object even close to leaving the solar system (it is on the edge in the heliosheath now, 8.7 billion miles from the sun), but it is probably fair to assume that other objects will follow in the next few hundred years.

However, from about 5,000 years B[efore]P[resent] humanities currently decipherable written records start, and these may well be our best hope for contacting an extraterrestrial species. If we confine ourselves to recorded history, statistically aliens are only 50 times more likely to have come in the last 5,000 years than in the last 100. This is a much smaller statistic, and not helped by the fact that this literature was only very sporadic for the first three thousand years! On the other hand, given the current political climate, where rich governments are testing weapons, aircraft and even space-planes (as for example the X37-B), there is very little transparency about what could be out there. This was not a problem before the twentieth century, and this alone might make the last figure I gave more tempting.

The Medieval Approach

> Year 676 – A marvellous star of great magnitude is seen
>
> shining through all the world.
>
> ('Annales Cambriae')

I am by no means the first person to advocate the study of ancient literature in search of aliens. The study owes much of its popularity, although not its genesis, to Erich von Däniken's *Chariots of the Gods* and various spin-offs. This book's most convincing evidence comes from Sanskrit literature. Sanskrit has many advantages for the modern investigator. Its corpus is massive, and there is a significant amount of engaging, fantastical and non-Christian (of course) storytelling. The corpus' oral nature also means that investigators are sometimes not required to answer clear questions about date and author. Indeed, so few people are conversant in the language (compared for example with Greek and Latin) that a researcher like Däniken can say things like:

> *'The fuel for this flying vehicle consisted of liquids, called 'madhu' and 'anna'; no Sanskrit scholars know how to translate these words.'* (*The Gods were Astronauts,* p.141)

And not be told to go and check the standard Sanskrit dictionary (Monier-Williams) to find that they are extraordinarily common words for 'honey' and 'food'.

Having said that however, no criticism of his language skills can refute his main finding, and the prevalence of the 'vimāna' (flying craft) motif has now been fully realised. Whether it is a freak coincidence that this Sanskrit motif has now resurfaced in literature of the modern Space-Age, or it suggests that both motifs are based on real physical phenomena is probably best left up to the individual to decide.

Similarly the late Zecharia Sitchin's *Earth Chronicles* series also searched through ancient literature. Over the course of his career, only finished by his death he sorted through the oldest literature from southern

Europe, the Near East, Egypt, and Mesoamerica and argued that humanity had been created by a race of astronauts from Nibiru (the twelfth planet), although his best work is on Babylonian texts. His books suffer from the opposite problem to Erich von Däniken's. Although his translations are generally better (although still unreliable) he takes the texts entirely literally, even if they are religious, mythical or fictional in nature. For example when he says:

> *Scholars are now hard put to explain why first the later Greeks and then the Romans assumed that Earth was flat, rising above a layer of murky waters below which there lay Hades or "Hell," when some of the evidence left by Greek astronomers from earlier times indicates that they knew otherwise.*
> (*The Twelfth Planet*, p.167)

The only scholar having any difficulty explaining this is himself. Actually the reason for the discrepancy is fairly obvious. The reason why the Greeks and Romans poetically spoke about Hades, and had stories about visits to the underworld is because they were not speaking scientifically at the time. In the same way, people in the modern day might speak to 'Our Father in Heaven' (even though 'heaven' originally just meant the sky) and make jokes about digging down through the other side of the Earth, even though scientifically they know that the Earth is too big for that. People would be corrected if they stated these things in an academic setting, but in context everyone understands that they are not trying to assert a scientific truth in their statement.

Sitchin also overanalyses anomalies within the texts and lets facts suit his theories rather than theories suit facts. For example he turns the mythical fight between Tiamat (a dragon) and Marduk (a god) into a story of how a planet was broken 4.5 billion years ago! However, for all the problems, his books *have* been phenomenally successful. He has single-handedly popularised Babylonian history and literature for millions of people and is even partially responsible for the 21st of December 2012 doomsday cult, despite never having made any predictions himself.

Generally though, the problem with ancient literature is that with some lurid exceptions, the vast bulk of the literature is mind-numbingly dull, and often religious, moral, economic or historic in nature. Researchers will be swamped with vast quantities of material of very little value to them, and be forced to search very hard for very little value. This makes it all too easy to overanalyse facts when they do arise. Also, the further back you go, the harder understanding the languages tend to be. Finally, before the fifteenth and sixteenth centuries in Europe, it is very hard to be sure of original date, and the identity and biases of the various authors and editors.

In the same way that those without advanced degrees in a subject rarely write about advanced physics or mathematics, and you would not trust their work if they did write about it, ancient literature has its own pitfalls, some of which I have highlighted above. It is best approached by an expert in the field, and most preferably a specialist, with a degree in the language or languages concerned.

I am far from a true expert in any strand of medieval literature, but I do at least have degrees in the subject. That is the reason why in this book I will be focusing on a single text at a time, fully (or extensively) translating each one, and putting each text in its context of time, place, manuscript source and genre, a task which would be very much more difficult for any researcher without specialist knowledge and language skills.

Medieval British literature

Before we begin, I should give an overview of the time period. The literature that we will be looking at occupies a very exciting period in history for the Earth in general and for Britain in particular, between 800 and 1400 A.D. For example, if we look just at Britain we see a time of great uncertainty and bloodshed. Politically, this is the time of Viking attacks and the foundation of the Danelaw (in North England) and the Kingdom of the Isles (of Scotland). The Picts and Scots of Scotland have united, and they annex Strathclyde, the last kingdom of Welsh-speakers in northern Britain. The Saxons, of Wessex, Mercia and Northumbria (the last two of which will not survive the period) who have been integrated with the Romanised Britons of these areas are at more-or-less constant war with the Scottish and Danes, not to mention the Welsh kingdoms and the Cornish, before the Normans arrive in 1066. Writing has long since been common, but writing in the vernacular languages instead of Latin starts around the beginning of this period, (although we have few manuscripts until its end). Deforestation on a massive scale and the draining of marshland means that humans are controlling the environment in a much more visible way, leading wild boar, beavers and even wolves to become rare, especially south of the wilderness of interior Scotland.

Map of Britain from immediately after the creation of the
"Danelaw" and the settling of the Vikings (around c. 878). The grey
territories in the west all speak an ancestor of Welsh (except Man,
France and Ireland). At this point that language would have been
spoken widely through the rest of the country as well, and would
have been the main language in Cornwall and Devon. The southern
territory is Saxon - Mercia and Wessex, along with the northern
territory of Northumbria. These places speak Old English. The central
territory of England is the Danelaw which speaks Norse.

Image created by Hel-hama and licensed under the Creative
Commons License.

The medieval Welsh language is the main source for our literature in
this book, and it includes the very earliest jottings in the Welsh language
up the literature of the fifteenth century. The language is Celtic and
therefore related to Irish. An ancestor of the current Welsh language
(British or Brittonic) was spoken in Britain, from the south-west tip of
Cornwall, and along the western sea-board of Britain as far north as
Edinburgh for at least a thousand years before the sixth-ninth century
AD. At the height of this period, British was the main language of the
entirety of Britain, and spoken even in lowland eastern England.
However the sixth-ninth centuries A.D. mark when Welsh, Cornish and
probably Cumbric (there is less evidence for this) "evolved" from their
common parent language (each spoken from then on only in their
respective areas), and the last Welsh kingdoms in Scotland and northern
England were lost. Sadly most of the literature from this period was also
lost, and what remains from this early period, with few exceptions, has
little to excite the investigator of the anomalous. However, this
language heritage has its effect on the literature. The medieval Welsh

generally call themselves (and the Cornish) Britons, their language is British, and in their legends of the "heroic age" these "Britons" tend to be the kings of Britain, if not always the only inhabitants. However, it is important to remember that since medieval welsh includes all the oldest Welsh material it is conceivable that some of this material may be much older than other parts.

This later Welsh of Wales is a much more varied hunting ground for accounts of the anomalous There are histories and annals of Britain with elements of the fantastic, there are religious catechisms, poetry of praise, elegies and satire for warriors, princes, places and upper-class patrons. Welsh literature was also probably the origin place for all medieval stories of King Arthur, which brings us to the so-called "traditional material". This resembles our modern fairy-tale genre, set in a magical world with mighty heroes. Within this genre there is a reoccurring feature, common to Welsh and Irish literature, of an otherworld, probably underground, peopled by a race of people who are eternally young and strong. Because some elements of this genre were believed in, even by rational people, it often provided a rationalisation for any events outside of the ordinary, while strange but true events were sometimes preserved as part of the genre. It therefore proves a very fertile, if dangerous source for researchers seeking aliens.

Latin was first spoken in Britain with the Roman influence at the turn of the millennium. However British "Vulgate" Latin (Latin spoken with a British accent) died out very soon after it started to develop when the Romans left and the inhabitants of the island starting using more and more British (the ancestor language of Welsh) again, even in the urban areas which weren't abandoned. On the other hand, the language was kept alive by the church, and it remained the language of scholarship, history and religion until the end of this period.

Old English (named after the Angles, of the Anglo-Saxons) developed either in England after the "invasion", or just before the "invaders" arrived. It has a smaller corpus than Welsh and may even be smaller than British Latin. However, the long heroic poems like Beowulf and Sir Gawain are unequalled in the other literatures.

Norman French and Old Norse are the last languages to arrive in Britain, and although they do leave some literature, it is often neither specific to Britain nor unique, and has only a limited relevance to Celtic literature.

Although I have made every effort to be accurate in my translations, I have at times needed to depart a little way from the exact wording of a sentence to make sure that the translation flows. My translations are also certainly not the equal to those of the scholarly geniuses who have furnished medieval literature with its greatest translations, although I hope they do accurately reflect what is written in the original language. Those lucky enough to know Welsh, or determined enough to slog through a dictionary can find the "editions" (tidied up versions of the original text) listed in the Introduction to each case, although I should caution that even native speakers of the modern language will find the older poetry very difficult. Even casual readers may occasionally wish to compare what I have written with what is written in another translation, and I have also listed these in the Introduction of each case. In particular readers may wish to have on hand a copy of *The Mabinogion*, which is the name of a modern anthology covering the majority of the medieval Welsh prose we will be examining in this book (not just the 'Four Branches of the Mabinogi'). Many different versions of this anthology are available, including some for free on *Project Gutenberg* and elsewhere. The version of *The Mabinogion* you are most likely to find is by Lady Charlotte Guest. Her version is fine for the most part, but readers should be aware that she skips over all of the "bedroom scenes" because of her Victorian sensibilities. Other than that small caveat, her translation, or anyone else's version of the text will be fine.

Literature Formatting Key	
Sample	**Explanation**
Special font	My direct translation from a medieval source.
'**Inverted commas**'	A quoted word or the name of a medieval source (other than a manuscript).
<u>**Underlined**</u>	A manuscript's name
Italics	Direct quotation from modern source.

[Square brackets]	My words, inserted into a direct quotation to help make sense.

A very approximate chronology

Before we begin properly I'd like to introduce the main sources which we'll be looking at. Generally any given "text" has an "probable" date assigned to it based on how old the language seems, and a "latest possible" date (T.A.Q.) according to the date of the manuscript it comes from. Since these dates are so debated, the following can only be termed a very approximate incomplete chronology. It presents the texts in approximately the right order, but the dates are merely estimates, informed by the scholarly consensus whenever possible:

800-900 A.D. (=the ninth century)
Downfall of Strathclyde, the last British kingdom outside of Wales other than Cornwall
Possible start of the "Old Welsh Period" under some classifications
'Historia Brittonum' written
Date of the language of 'Y Gododdin' (original poem may be from the sixth or seventh century)
Date of the language of the "historic" 'Poems of Taliesin'
First version of 'The Anglo Saxon Chronicle' is compiled up to 892 from older sources

900-1000 A.D. (=the tenth century)
Approximate date for 'Beowulf'
Earliest possible language date for 'Preiddeu Annwfn'
Earliest language date for 'Poems of Llywarch Hen' and attendant saga englynion
Date for first part of 'Annales Cambriae'
Date of The Exeter Codex (source of most Old English poems mentioned)

1000-1100 A.D. (=the eleventh century)
Approximate of the Nowell Codex (source of Beowulf)
Approximate date of 'Culhwch'
Approximate date of the earliest version of 'The Mabinogi' ('Pwyll', 'Branwen', 'Manawydan', 'Math')

1100-1200 A.D. (=the twelfth century)
Approximate date of 'Lludd a Llefelys'

Date of the <u>Peterborough Chronicle</u> (one version of the 'Anglo Saxon
Chronicle') and its final entries
Date of 'Historia Regum Britanniae'
Probable date of 'Rhonabwy'
Date of Chretien de Troyes' Romances

1200-1300 A.D. (=the thirteenth century
Start of the "Middle Welsh" Period
Approximate date of Welsh Romances ('Owain', 'Geraint', 'Peredur')
The <u>Black Book of Caerfyrddin</u> is written
<u>Peniarth 6</u> (Containing fragments of 'the Mabinogi') written
<u>Peniarth 7</u> (containing part of 'Peredur' and 'Geraint') written
<u>Hendregadredd Manuscript</u> is written
<u>Llanstephan 1</u> (containing 'Lludd a Llefelys') is written

1300-1350 A.D. (=the first half of the fourteenth century)
<u>Book of Taliesin</u> written
<u>Book of Aneirin</u> (containing 'Y Gododdin') written

1350-1400 (=the second half of the fourteenth century)
<u>White Book of Rhydderch</u> (containing almost all stories now found in
The Mabinogion) written
<u>Red Book of Hergest</u> (containing all the stories found in *The Mabinogion*[4]
) written
'Marwnad Ithel ap Robert' and other Cywyddwyr poems written

1400-1500 (=the fifteenth century)
<u>Peniarth 51</u> written (a composition of the 'Thirteen Treasures of the Isle
of Britain')

As you have probably noticed, the surviving manuscripts (<u>underlined</u>)
are in almost all cases very much earlier than the texts ('in inverted
commas'). This is quite normal for literature, although even the oldest
mainly-Welsh language manuscripts we have are later than the Old
English and Irish manuscripts. Most texts earlier that the twelfth century

---

[4] All the texts included in the standard anthology of medieval Welsh prose (*the
Mabinogion*) are found in the <u>Red Book</u> except the poems of Taliesin (which are
included in Lady Charlotte Guest's version).

probably had their origin in the oral tradition, made famous by Celtic "bards"[5]. There probably were manuscripts by the twelfth century, although modern scholarship would call any extant purely Welsh manuscript dating from 1250-1350 "early".

In these texts we are especially looking for motifs and topoi which either contain 'marvels' which can be explained by modern science or specifically describe contact with an alien race. Obviously many of these motifs and topoi are deeply embedded in Welsh literature. Stories of contact with other races are not contemporary, but often set in accounts from the (mainly fictional) heroic age. Separating a kernel of fact from the fiction it inspired is a very difficult job, and made even harder since any historical reality reflected in these stories as a cultural memory is likely to be very old indeed.

So how long can an oral, cultural memory endure? Could our medieval motifs and topoi be centuries of even one thousand years old? It is possible. There are some cultural continuities for example, between Britain in the present day and Britain in the time of the Norman Conquest of 1066. Likewise, north of the Hebrides there is a small island called Sula Sgeir. Every year, men from Nis, a port in the far north of Lewis go to this rock, and spend a few weeks hunting 'gugaichean' (young gannets). They salt these and bring them back to be eaten in the community throughout the year. A record from 1546 attests that hunters had been going on expeditions to this rock each year for two hundred years before that point, although in those times the people were probably hunting eider-ducks rather than gannets. The "Uffington Beast" in Britain is a chalk figure, commonly thought to be a White Horse, which can be seen on a hill near Oxford. Unlike most of the other chalk figures which can still be found in Britain, this one does actually date back to the Bronze Age. Optically stimulated luminescence testing was used in 1995 and found a date 1380-550 B.C. or 2915 B.P. (before present) ±415. The Uffington Beast could not have been ignored either. Up until the mid-nineteenth century it must have been "scoured" frequently by the locals to stop it becoming overgrown with weeds and to replace the chalk washed away by soil leeching and rain. Records from the seventeenth to nineteenth centuries suggest it was scoured at

[5] The word 'bardd' in Welsh can denote any poet, but by the late medieval period it tends to refer specifically to a low grade of professional poet

a local fair every seven years. Although the scourers of the nineteenth century had no idea when the beast was created, or who it was created by, they were still scouring it. Finally, the example of survival closest to our subject is that of 'Y Gododdin'. This is probably the earliest Welsh poem (possibly written in Scotland) and describes events that occurred at the end of the sixth century Battle of Catraeth, but its earliest surviving manuscript is from the fourteenth. Although the poem was re-worded with the changing of the language, and details were added, essentially the plot would have been still recognisable. All of these are examples of cultural survivals. If we need only motifs and topoi to survive, we may be looking very far back indeed.

The case of 'Marwnad Ithel ap Robert'

Introduction

At the beginning of this book I gave Fergus Kelly's thoughts on the strange disease which struck Connacht after the death of Cathal Crobhdearg Ua Conchobair. Although that particular sickness was not recorded by any annalists in Britain, and Britain has no sickness with such striking similarity to radiation to match it, the events described in Marwnad Ithel ap Robert (the Elegy of Ithel, son of Robert) must surely be a trump for British literature. It was written by Iolo Goch (Iolo the Red) who was one of the most famous of the 'cywyddwyr', the professional poets who sang praises to their patrons, often promising immortality in verse in return for payment in gold or gifts of fine clothes, horses or livestock. He wrote this poem for his old patron, an archdeacon, in the fourteenth century, making this one of the very latest of our texts. It draws on a series of freak events which happened at the time to show how holy Ithel was, and how sad his death is. Although this is a clear manipulation of his material by Iolo Goch, we have to wonder whether the events could in fact still be linked, even if they are not (all) triggered by the death of Ithel.

Since the text is so late, we are in the enviable position of knowing exactly who wrote it, and what it is about. However, this does not mean there are no difficulties with it, as we shall see. There is a Welsh edition by Saunders Lewis in *Ysgrifau Beirniadol iii,* but the standard edition of the text is in Eurys Rowlands' (1976) *Poems of the Cywyddwyr*. There are two excellent translations, *Poems of Iolo Goch* and Joseph Clancy's *Medieval Welsh Poems* (these vary in line order).

This translation of the text and some of the discussion (although not the interpretation) was published in the 'Journal of Anomalous Sciences, April-June 2012' edition. Full permission has been obtained to reprint it.

The Text

1.

The breaking of the earth is strange

Now shoots of plague

And strange the breeding of terror

On it, a deep, dripping globe

There is trembling (a cold shivering fear)

And the ague (a hot-fit of fever)

A storm came, it is Tuesday

A great day between the ending of March

And April (unprofitable for us)

Thursday was a beginning of horror

Between the new day and the night

Few know what [its] cause [was]

Ithel ap Robert died in 1382, and this was the same year that a powerful earthquake hit Britain, (a very rare occurrence). There was also plague in this year (a much more common occurrence in fourteenth century Britain). The interest for our purposes comes in the author putting all of these things together. Iolo almost seems to be suggesting that the plague sprouted from the broken earth like a plant from a ploughed field. This has disconcerting parallels with our earlier discussion of Annwfn, but Annwfn is not usually depicted as a place hostile to humans.

Fever and chills are symptoms of all kinds of plague, but they are also, of course, quite common symptoms of other illnesses too. Other accounts suggest that this illness may have only affected children (see: A History of Epidemics in Britain, pp.218-19). Therefore this plague was probably not a resurgence of bubonic plague (black death). The reference to a 'deep, dripping, globe' therefore is unlikely to refer to buboes (swollen lymph nodes). It may refer to the world itself (the spherical shape of the world was written about in Britain by Bede centuries earlier) but this would be unique in my experience of Welsh literature. The great storm referred to may refer to the rebellion of Dafydd ap Gruffydd against English control of Wales on the 29th of March 1282, although this was a Sunday. Perhaps whatever this storm was, it is more likely to have come two days later on Tuesday, the 31st of March 1282.

The repetition of the word 'eres' (strange) supplies an overall feeling to the verse that something rather unusual is happening, an idea which is confirmed by the final line of the verse, and suggests (i) that there was a cause for these disasters and (ii) that the poet knows what this cause was.

2

A great blow the dying of Ithel

Son of Robert, (a pretty boy, a generous boy)

Who gave to us broad red-gold

and silver and gold

A magical stone of lustrous passion

A pure great, splendid pearl

Valuable jewel of [the] Angelic Eingl,

A pure, good, fair, butterfly of Tegeingl,

A friend of his land, ruler of feasting

Holy cross and soul of Gwynedd

Brother to an angel, youthful mind

[With] every wrong and right, all that he attempts

No-one may pass judgement on him

There is blame that he did not survive

Verse two is mostly given over to praise of Ithel, but for our circumstances there is some interest in all of the amazing holy artefacts and relics. First, the 'Croes Naid' is a historically attested fragment of the true cross enclosed within a cross and kept in Gwynedd until it was taken in the conquest of Wales probably quite soon after this poem was written. It has since been lost, and has probably been destroyed but its general outline is remembered to resemble a Celtic cross.

The 'Eingl' could be the Angles commonly supposed to have settled Britain along with the Saxons (although this reference would then be very anachronistic), Saunders Lewis in his edition suggested (p.16) that it should rather refer to the inhabitants of Tegeingl (Flintshire), mentioned in the next line, but as Dr. Rowlands said in her edition (p.66), this name for the inhabitants is not otherwise attested. Finally, this is also the word used for an angel from heaven (also mentioned a few lines later). If the gem was reputed to belong to angels (it is certainly 'angelic' at least), what manner of stone is it? 'Magical stones' are found elsewhere in Celtic literature. Perhaps most famously there is one in Breuddwyd Ronabwy' (The Dream of Rhonabwy) which King Arthur wears in Rhonabwy's dream. This one allows Rhonabwy to remember his lucid dream, which he would otherwise forget, a very strange property for a gem. This only leaves more questions though. Where would Ithel have acquired such a gem? Was it directly from the 'Eingl' of Tegeingl? If so, what does this suggest? Saunders Lewis (p.24) suggests this is a metaphor for Ithel. Certainly we are talking *about* Ithel by the end of this description, but surely the broad red gold is something given *by* Ithel. The pearl comes directly between these descriptions so could be interpreted either way.

3.

There has not yet been of the world

[The] same generous sea as this one dying

Woe to those singers in wind and rain

And [to the] earth after the blackening

There has not been [another] like this one, however short

it may be

A storm nor any weather

Compared to [the] unreal, wrong [tempest of] today

Like this, woe [for] my tall Lord

Stanza three continues the praise of Ithel, but also explains how strange the storm was in more detail, and compares it to other storms. This perhaps suggests that the storm was an actual terrible storm rather than the start of the rebellion I mentioned earlier as Welsh uprisings were common up to this time, not unique like this storm.

'Mor hael' (generous sea) is a common stock praise epithet. The 'dduaw' (blackening) of the 'ddaer' (earth/ The Earth) seems strange to me though. Could it be a reference back to the earthquake? If so, why would an earthquake blacken the earth?

4.

Holy God (it was agreed)

For the sake of the praise of the thousand thousands

He became manifest like he did

After suffering, it was good

When he fell, [to] a gigantic false [place]

The harrowing of hell, a desolate marsh

And shaking, oh from the cold

From the wide, pure, grey earth

Then he sent Jesus -

Back, he was his beloved son

And a host of angels like this

Voicing psalms, voice of lively rulers

And good, solemn litanies

Verse four seems strange at first sight, but is actually rather simple to explain. The verse is comparing Ithel's death, which was accompanied by earthquake, plague and storms with Jesus' death which, according to the Bible, was accompanied by an earthquake, an eclipse, the resurrection of many people and the tearing of the curtain in the synagogue (see Matthew 27;45-53). By comparing the two, Iolo Goch brings greater praise to Ithel, who is thus given an almost divine status. Importantly, this verse also mentions Jesus being accompanied by a host of angels on his way either back to earth or to heaven (from the harrowing of hell).

5

Now, no less the tumult

That came together, before the prime

To bring the worthy, fair body

Of the apostle, without pause

Of wise-men, there has n[ever] come together

[An equal to] the amount on this island [now]

This made the weather cold

Taking rain from the hard-moon

The black earth, sending forth dust

Shaking, how great was the trembling

Mother of every warm fertile crop

Mantle of cold from the size of its load

When they made for, (a fragile dream)

To the holy church of incense

Verse five is the one in which the most anomalous things start to happen. First of all I should point out that this verse starts with a 'twrwf' (tumult, strange loud sound). In this case it probably refers literally to the singing which follows Ithel to his grave, just like the singing of angels which followed Jesus. However, this suggests a comparison between the 'wise men' in this verse, and 'Eingl' in the last. In addition, please see "Cases of Strange Sounds", for an explanation of how a 'twrwf' usually precedes a strange event in literature. A great retinue of wise men, the like of which has never been seen, arrived on this island (a common name for Britain). This is recorded as a historical fact in a prose note after the text in the Peniarth 72 manuscript (85), which mentions that there were a great number of people present including mounted men, men on foot, three monasteries [of monks], sermon-givers, men in mantles and two bishops. All this seems very normal, if hyperbolic, but Iolo seems to equate the natural disasters he has been describing with their arrival. He says explicitly: 'hyn a wnaeth yr hin yn oer' (this made the weather cold), and indeed brought a 'mantell oer' (mantle of cold ?=snow?) over the world. Their arrival took 'adlaw' (a less usual form of 'glaw', rain) from the 'caledloer' (hard-moon). We also see another reference to 'ddaer ddu' (black earth/Earth). Could the blackening mentioned earlier have been caused by the arrival of so many people like the strange rain and the cold weather? Other poets sometimes refer to a 'planed ddu' (black planet), which seems to be a baleful sign in the sky which may perhaps be related. All these people came together before the prime hour (six o' clock A.M.) and made for the church, presumably to witness Ithel's funeral.

6

From Coed-y-mynydd with him

And his whole household mourning

Many a squire behind

Shouting constantly, woe to the weak

Many tears on women's cheeks

Many a cold nephew, many a niece

Many a consequence of [his] long-life

Oh me, that he may not be well [and] alive

Many a loud cry, with bell and voice

And a scream until evening prayer time

Around the body in purple

Singing, inhabiting the choir

And they walked from the saints [church?] and ran

A funeral party, a fair convent

Verse six has little to interest us, and only describes a dream open-casque funeral-procession of the time. Loud lamentation was probably typical of funerals of the time, and is frequently mentioned in the literature (compare Gaelic 'caoineadh' (keening) traditions). Coed-y-mynydd (forest of the mountain) is unfortunately a rather common name, and could refer to multiple locations.

This scene from the Bayeaux Tapestry depicts the funeral of Edward the Confessor (over three hundred years earlier). The casket is open, just like in Ithel's case, and the body is being taken to a church. The tapestry makers have depicted less people than were seen at Ithel's funeral, but this is probably to save space rather than from any lack of regard. The crowd shows the same combination of close family bearing him, nobles and (little) monks with bells, but Edward is destined for a sarcophogus, whereas Ithel was buried.

7

Woe of two-thousand after he comes

From inside the church, (handsome fame)

And hearing, grievous the tumult

Bells and meandering of clerics and bewailing

And light, woe of many

Three [times?] more, than a ?constellation? of stars

Of bright flaming torches of flaming wax

Like lanterns of fire, complete vigorous lightning

More than anything was [the number] in the temple

Of the stately gentlemen, fitting of the multitude

In verse seven more strange things happen. The funeral procession arrives at the church, and inside the church, the people are 'mwy na dim' (more than anything). There is a confusion of clerics bells (priests often carried bells in medieval times) and very bright light. 'Serlwy' is an usual word, and Rowlands tentatively suggests 'constellation' as a translation (p.68). 'Gwae lawer' (woe of many) I take to be just an interjection of sadness. This poet seems to find this light hard to describe. The first line suggests that it might by another hyperbolic utterance referring to the number of people present with torches, like the people who bring lighters and candles to current church services. This would be easy to understand, given that the last verse explained that their journey to the church took until evening. However even two thousand torches would not have lit up a cathedral big enough to hold their bearers inside, never mind the small likelihood that 2,000 people would be allowed to bring unmasked wax torches inside a pre-reformation church with its ornamentation. Therefore I take 'of bright flaming torches of flaming wax' to be a metaphor, like the simile in the line afterwards, trying to describe the confusing bright light in the church. What could have caused this strange light, which is compared with the brightest things which the poet can imagine? Something must have caused the night-time to brighten like lightning. Could it have something to do with the strange number of people present? At the least the final description of the retinue as 'gwyrda beilch' (stately good-men) may be significant for understanding the identity of this host of people.

Photo released into the public domain by John Armagh. St Asaph Cathedral is one of the two main medieval cathedrals in Gwyned, and this picture shows one corner of its cruciform shape.

8

Some squeezing fingers, a sad sight

Great terror like a dying grip

Maidens, of dear esteem

Some fainting, others swooning

Some pulling [hair from the] top of both sides [of their

head]

And head hair like straw [on the] floor

And paupers, sorrowful men

Howling strongly

The cross-shaped church rocked

With the tumult and the solemn clamour

Like a spacious ship to anchor

Withered, it will tremble on [the] sea

Verse eight continues with a description of how upset his funeral attendants seem to be, with hyperbolic descriptions of their grief. The squeezing of fingers may be a reference to what we in English would call the wringing of hands. The end of the verse has something of interest for us however as the church (most British churches are cruciform) begins to rock like a ship at anchor. Is this the earthquake mentioned earlier?

9

Woe to you Iolo, woe to his family

From the gold robes to the black pit

Throwing fine stones or gravel

Above him, wall of covering;

And many shouts, great intent

All around him like there was a battle

Well known in every court and church

The breaking of the earth into three-pieces

Verse nine seems to refer to Ithel's burial, with the attendant grievers. Again we have a reference to what seems to be an earthquake, and we can only complain that the fact of the matter wasn't recorded by a few more 'Ilys a llan' (court and church).

10

Wrong the shouting over [him]

For a man like he, heaven to us

After he had, generous old age

He is accepted by God and [the] state

Better silence than rough shouting

Painful loss, of [lit: at] a fine-stag

Behold, [what] was good for him

Worship to Christ, without mourning

Giving a resting place, a good happening

For his soul, he was a Lamb of God

With Elijah, walking saint

And Enoch in glory

The two solemn saints will not come

(They are brothers from paradise)

If he may not come, his time of the right[-hand]

Judgement-day in the final judgement

There will not be on the top of fortune Mount

Of Olives, perfect, purple

A Lord archdeacon fairer

Than Ithel of high lineage shall be.

Iolo Goch our poet seems to have become fed up of his own hyperbolic use of the grievers by this point, and reproves those screaming for not being quieter. He finishes with the typical medieval Christian suggestion that others should live holy and dignified lives. He also compares Ithel to Elijah and Enoch. These two are significant in that they were famously both physically taken up to heaven on chariots of fire without having to die. There is no hint of this happening to Ithel at this time, but the poet does seem to be suggesting that the strange things that have happened are because of Ithel's holiness. Iolo Goch finishes by insisting that neither of these saints will come to heaven (presumably on the day of final judgement) unless Archdeacon Ithel is allowed to come with them, and he will be the fairest archdeacon there on that day.

Interpretation

In my opinion, if the events of Marwnad Ithel ap Robert were repeated today, an alien explanation would be very quickly offered, and it is only the age, context, and peoples expectations of the text which mean that the explanation has not been offered before now. To sum up the sequence of events, the author, Iolo Goch describes an earthquake, plague and great storm in 1282 (verse 1). He also describes the arrival of a retinue of 'wise', 'stately' gentlemen (5, 7), which is so large that it seems to 'make the earth black', and 'send forth dust' (3, 5), brings an earthquake, and makes the weather cold (5). This retinue goes to the church to watch Ithel be buried (nearby/under the floor?) at which point there is a strange great light (7) and earthquake (8).

Occam's Razor suggests that the simplest explanations which require the least assumptions are probably the most likely to be correct. Consider two scenarios: In the first, a strong earthquake (the like of which is seen only once or twice in a hundred years in Britain) and storm (perhaps slightly more common) both occur in the same year. Also in that year there is plague, which is not an uncommon occurrence at this point, and could maybe have been caused by damaged sewers left by the earthquake like after the 1906 San Francisco earthquake. Following this a drought kills all the crops, and even some of the trees in an area (probably at least as rare as the earthquake in a Welsh climate), leaving the area coated in bare soil which turns to dust. In winter this is covered in snow, and we assume the exaggeration of the numbers present, and the strange bright light are poetic innovations by Iolo Goch. This scenario is not completely out of the question but seems very unlikely.

In the second scenario, whether to witness the funeral of Ithel ap Robert, or for another reason, an alien spacecraft lands in Britain. The landing is very hard, and leads to an earthquake[6], which unleashes a plague in the same way as before. Then a 'strange', 'unreal' storm is

---

[6] This idea has definite parallels: a mini-earthquake was created by the 1974 Cader Bronwen incident where something crashed into the side of a Welsh mountain very close to the setting of this poem, and in the Bible Matthew chapter 28 verse 2 specifically records how an angel coming down from heaven caused an earthquake.

created by the movement of the ship through the atmosphere, or possibly the ship refuelling[7]. The blackening of the earth is caused by the ship either landing or taking off (witness the ground underneath a NASA takeoff). In this case though, either the ship is very big, or there are multiple ships, which sends up a dust cloud. This goes up into the atmosphere for a few days and partially obscures the sun, making it cold. No snow falls, but the dust falls down over the next few days as white ash. The white light on the funeral can easily be explained as the arrival of another ship, or simply a ship turning on its lights to stun the crowd. Iolo could be completely right that the arrival of the 'gentlemen' did cause all of these things.

NASA Expedition 32. Note the launch-pad blackening caused by the rocket fuel.

To me, although the events described are hard to imagine, the second scenario seems to involve far less coincidences. One cause, the arrival of the 'gentlemen' in a space ship, would explain everything that happened except the plague and the colder climate, which are both

---

[7] This idea also has definite parallels: UFOs are very commonly seen during electric storms and there is some suggestion in medieval Welsh legends that the arrival of supernatural characters causes storms or just loud sounds – see my chapter "Cases of Strange Sounds" for more discussion.

triggered indirectly. If an alien explanation is not to be rejected immediately as too far-fetched, then it actually becomes the most probable explanation. This however leads to more questions. The first is why the aliens came.

Iolo Goch's implicit explanation for their arrival is that they came because Ithel is so holy like Jesus, he juxtaposes their arrival with his verse about Jesus being guided by angels, and probably meant his audience to view them in this light. I reject that explanation, but I do not believe that the events may be related to Ithel ap Robert. Verse 2 spoke of the 'magical stone... jewel of the Angelic Eingl' (engylfawr Eingl), whether this is a metaphor for Ithel ap Robert, or something which he gave to his people, either way it suggests a friendship with the Eingl. And if they are not simply the Angles, or the inhabitants of Tegeingl, it may well be that this was a name for an alien species.

Certainly the 'Eingl' seem quite friendly. Like the Irish Sí and the Welsh people of Annwfn, these aliens physically resemble humans enough to be praised as good examples of the race. It seems quite possible that they were also involved in mourning him, in which case we can ascribe the gentlemen very human emotions. On the other hand, if they triggered all of these natural disasters in their wake, this suggests either a lack of fore-knowledge of how their ship would affect the world, or a lack of compassion about what happens to humans (possibly other than Ithel). From humanities point of view this is a worrying trait in an alien species, and mirrors the lack of concern in answering, and lack of regard for human life probably demonstrated by the tower/fort in the Case of 'Preiddeu Annwfn'.

The Case of 'Preiddeu Annwfn'

Introduction

'Preiddeu Annwfn' (The Spoils of the Underworld) is a poem found in the thirteenth century <u>Book of Taliesin</u>. The material of this codex is the subject of much contention between scholars. In medieval times it was believed that much or all of the material in this book was the work of Taliesin, a poet from the sixth century. Taliesin probably was a real poet and probably did write around that time (he is mentioned in other early texts like 'Y Gododdin', and his name was recorded, along with Aneirin's, as one of great poets of past times in *Historia Brittonum*, which was written 828-30, and drew on older material. In fact, the difficulty with Taliesin comes simply because of his fame. Scholars of Welsh are now fairly certain that much of the material attributed to him, particularly the prose-legends about him were created much later, and attributed to him either by the authors, wanting to see their work preserved, or by confused scribes who saw his name as a "convenient peg" on which to hang any old looking or strange (especially prophetic) material. Poets and scribes were more than capable of purposefully writing in an older orthographic form of their language, and also modernising older poems as they copied, which makes it incredibly difficult to separate out "authentic" and "inauthentic" strands. This means that 'Preiddeu Annwfn' can only be dated based on the form we have, which is written in the Old Welsh language and dated to 850-1250, and we can't be sure who wrote it, although it is highly unlikely to have been the historic Taliesin's work, since he was more interested in eulogy and elegy. Further, even if Arthur had been conceived by this point (a debated topic), if Taliesin claimed to have gone on a sea-voyage with him he would have been laughed at, since Arthur even in the earliest times was a figure from out of legend. I believe we must therefore view this text as deliberate "fiction". This poem was probably set by someone in the heroic age with Arthur, rather than written by anybody actually in a heroic age.

The subject matter of this poem is extraordinary. An expedition, led by [King] Arthur goes to Annwfn. They leave in what we assume is a ship called 'Prydwen' (white shape/face) and either make multiple journeys, or put three times more men on the ship than would normally fit. This echoes a very old genre of literature in medieval Ireland called the *Immram*, where a hero crosses the sea and finds the otherworld in a ship. However, this is the only voyage tale found in medieval Welsh literature and as such it seems very unusual. There is no hint that the ship should be regarded as anything strange, and it expressly travels 'on the sea' (unlike the vimāna motif in Sanskrit literature for example) but there are certain other strange artefacts we shall discuss as they appear. The poem suggests that their voyage was very dangerous since only seven returned. The text also suggests a few reasons they might have gone on the voyage – a man called Gweir is imprisoned there, and there is an otherworldly cauldron and a sword (discussed further in "Cases of Powerful Artefacts") which may be the "preiddeu" (spoils/loot) mentioned in the title.

Annwfn, (the otherworld/underworld) in Welsh (and Irish) medieval literature is usually described as under the earth or on an island across the sea. Although the standard modern Welsh spelling is 'Annwn' I have used 'Annwfn' since the medieval understanding of the word is not quite the same as the modern one. It was probably originally a compound of 'ann' (in) and 'dwfn' (earth). This second element loses its 'd' entirely naturally and according to one of the Celtic languages' complex mutation rules (nasalisation). Based on the name therefore, we can see that Annwfn was probably originally thought to be underground, and this is the way it is described in most texts. Its presence across seas is rarer and possibly attributable to Irish influence. In late medieval Welsh texts it just refers to anything going deep under the earth, like a fox's earth in Dafydd ap Gwilym's 'The Fox'.

A final interesting point to make before we begin is the role of Arthur in the text. In the earliest Welsh texts we find Arthur as a hero and warrior rather than a king or emperor, and that is the case in this text as well. The appearance of Arthur, magic artefacts, (i.e. mythic) and overtly religious material are all signs that the text should be considered as quite late in date, even though the language suggests it is very early.

The standard edition and translation is found in *Legendary Poems from the Book of Taliesin* by Marged Haycock. In this poem I have split up the verses based on the end rhyme of the Welsh edition. Since this coincides with the use of the refrain the verse pattern is probably original.

The Text

1.

I worship the Lord, the Prince, King of Land

Who has extended his rule across the shore of the world

Gweir's prison in Sidi Fortress was complete

through the gospel of Pwyll and Pryderi

No-one went to it sooner than he

The heavy blue chain [was] a true servant that held him

And before the spoils of Annwfn bitterly he sang

And to the judgement our bard-prayer endured

[In] thrice-filled Prydwen we went to it

Except seven, none returned from Sidi Fortress

The most interesting thing about verse one is the name repeated twice, 'Caer Sidi' (Sidi Fortress). Sidi is an interesting word and almost certainly a borrowing from the Old Irish. There 'Síd' is usually translated as 'fairy-mound', but with an Old Irish appreciation of "fairy" as a 'person from the otherworld'. Old Irish "fairies" (sí) are depicted as strong, attractive, wise, immortal youths (male and female). This translation agrees well with the setting of the poem, which we already know is Annwfn (the Welsh otherworld). As I said earlier, the presence of the otherworld across the seas in this text may well suggest additional Irish influence.

I should also point out that hardly any of the names which appear to be used for God in this poem are normal. The titles used in the first line for example 'gwledic', 'pendeuic' 'gwlat ri' are all words more normally used to describe (grand) human rulers. Nevertheless, the context of worship makes it clear that the poet is referring to the Christian God, as we see especially in verse 7, where the line is half repeated and the name 'crist' (Christ) also features. Perhaps this is deliberate archaising by a scribe.

This verse has material which may derive from 'Y Gododdin' and various other sources. This includes the prisoner motif, which in 'Y Gododdin' has Aneirin composing the poem overnight, chained in an underground prison. He is only rescued the next day by Cenau, son of Llywarch Hen. This is clearly a late interpolation to the text however, as throughout the rest of the poem a periodic refrain is that 'only one returned'. This refrain, incidentally, is very reminiscent of the last line of the verse above, offering another point of influence between the texts.

Returning to the chained prisoner motif, another famous prisoner is Mabon, son of Modron whose tale is told in an episode of 'Culhwch ac Olwen'. He is similarly bound in chains and imprisoned underground, from the day he is three days old, under Loyw Fortress. More famous prisoners are named in the triadic material, but the similarities between these stories should be enough to suggest how common a motif it is.

Pwyll and Pryderi are characters from the 'Mabinogi'. Pryderi is Pwyll's son, and the only character to play a role on all four of the 'branches' (parts). Both of the characters were friendly with Arawn, the Lord of the Otherworld, thus the Gospel of Pwyll and Pryderi could be the 'Mabinogi' itself, or perhaps just a reference to how Gweir became imprisoned.

2.

I am [of] splendid fame, my song is heard

In the four-cornered fortress [from all] four-sides

My first word, from the cauldron when it was spoken

From breath of nine maidens it was kindled

It is the cauldron of the Head of Annwfn; what is its

nature?

A collar about the rim with pearls

It does not boil coward's food (that has not been fated)

To it Lluch Lleawch's sword has been raised

And in the hand of Leminawc it was left

And before the entrance-gate of hell lanterns burned

And when we went with Arthur (terrific toil)

Except seven none returned from Medwit Fortress

Verse two is much more difficult to explain than the previous one. I interpret the first four lines as the poet's boast. His song is so loud it is heard all around a large fortress, and his voice is as sweet as nine maidens. If the singer is Taliesin, this would explain why his first word was from the cauldron, as Taliesin, like Fionn MacCumhail, in the late legends written acquired his awen (poetic inspiration) from a drop from the cauldron of knowledge. However the words 'from the cauldron' may just refer to especially true or poetic words, the expression is also used in the poem 'In Praise of Llywelyn ap Iorwerth'. The last three lines are equally quite clear, and suggest that after Arthur and his companions went on their ship, they may have gone underground to find the entrance to the otherworld; hell is certainly underground in medieval Christian cosmography, and the darkness, and lanterns are more explainable if the voyagers are not outside. The Fortress at the end of this verse seems to be just another name for the underworld fortress which is our main subject. 'Medwit' refers to mead-drunkenness, and is quite a positive name (mead was quite a high status drink and few could afford to get drunk on it).

The central five lines of this verse describe two strange artefacts, the 'peir pen annwfyn' (cauldron of the Head of Annwfn) and 'Cledyf Lluch Lleawch'. Koch and Carey render this last 'a sword of lightning's slaughter'. This is probably originally what it the name meant, and describes the nature of the sword, but the term would probably have been understood as a proper name more than a description by the time this poem was written. Both of these artefacts are mentioned elsewhere and have their own mythology which I shall describe in my interpretation of this poem later on.

3.

I am [of] splendid fame, my song is heard

In the four-cornered fortress (strong-door of the island)

Brightest day and jet-[black] are mixed

Bright wine their drink, before their retinue

[In] thrice-filled Prydwen, we went on the sea

Except seven, none returned from Rigor Fortress

Verse three gives some more details of the fortress, here called the fortress of 'Rigor' (literally 'of numbness' - not the English word 'rigour'). The four-cornered fortress we had in the last verse is now revealed to be 'ynys pebyrdor' (strong-door of the island), which suggests it is a sort of gatehouse, perhaps synonymous with the entrance gate of hell given above. To my mind this suggests an island with a large fortress, through which one descends to enter Annwfn (explaining the laterns in the last verse, and the jet-blackness of this verse), although I'm not sure what the explanation for the brightest day could be. If the fortress must stand alone it could perhaps refer to a submarine, and we shall discuss this idea further later. The line after that is very much reminiscent of a few lines in 'Y Gododdin', the poem I mentioned earlier, so this may well be a stray line, attracted to the verse because of similarity of the rhyme (a common occurrence). The final verse repeats for the second time the refrain which we will now get at the end of each verse until the last.

4.

I do not deserve small men of the Lord's literature

Beyond Gwydyr Fortress they did not see the valour of Arthur

Three-score hundred men stood on the wall

Speech with their watchman was hard

Thrice-filled Prydwen went with Arthur

Except seven, none returned from Golud Fortress

Verse four contains, for me, some of the most interesting points of the entire poem. The first line seems to refer to monks and clerics, and suggests that the author deserves a better audience than he has. This is a very unusual boast given the power of the Christian church throughout the medieval period, and becomes stronger as the poem continues, becoming most almost a tirade against the ignorance and uselessness of monks in verses six and seven.

The second line is ambiguous. It has usually been taken to agree with the fourth line, suggesting that the men on Prydwen are so far from civilised parts that they did not recognise Arthur. This is quite possible given the following lines, but there is an alternative explanation. 'Gwydyr' (mutated to 'Wydyr' in the text) is the normal word for 'glass' and this word is also found, in a slightly different form, in 'Ynys Wydrin' (Gwydrin Island). This is a name commonly assigned to Glastonbury, an old medieval abbey which is now a town in Somerset, in south west England. The first use of that name is difficult to pin down. It was probably mentioned in Caradoc's 'Vita Gildae', written in 1135 and again by Gerald of Wales in 1194. The name may be older than this however, as it is also quoted in William of Malmesbury's 'De Antiquitate Glastoniensis Ecclesiae' as part of a charter from 601, as well as in another quite old Welsh poem, 'Ymddiddan Gwenhwyfar ac Melwas', and in French Arthurian tales which mention Melwas. Dating aside, most scholars doubt that these two names are anything but a strange coincidence. However if we allow 'tra' (beyond) to have the force of 'nam' (apart from, except for), which it usually cannot have, then this name could possibly refer to Glastonbury. Glastonbury Abbey claimed to have discovered Arthur's body in 1215, and included many eyewitness accounts. Allowing a date very late in the Old Welsh window allowed for this text, this line could have the force of 'other than Glastonbury, monks haven't been concerned with Arthur's valour' or 'monks haven't cared about Arthur except for his being found at Glastonbury'. However this would be pushing the translation a bit far, and would necessitate a very late date for a text which (for example) uses the Older Celtic remnant 'ri' rather than 'brenhin' the medieval Welsh standard. Perhaps the former suggestion is therefore more likely.

The third and fourth lines are very often quoted, and they really do emphasise the difference between the people of the Sidi Fortress and Arthur's men from Britain. Three-score hundred makes 6,000, and this is a very large amount of people to garrison any one fortress. 'Breuddwyt Ronabwy' gives a good comparison. This story is set partially in twelfth century Wales and in this part, Powys is put on guard and one hundred people are set for each three "commotes" in the province. Considering there were only around eleven commotes in the province at this time, this means that 400 people patrolled the entire area. The exact boundaries of the area are hard to establish, but it was probably similar to that of the modern preserved county, which is over 5000km (3107 miles)[2]. This may well be a purposefully small number, used because that text was set in a "heroic past" when matters were simpler. However the idea of 6,000 men guarding a wall still seems quite a considerable exaggeration.

The fourth line is even more interesting. In Britain in the past, most people were multilingual, and so to find any special difficulty talking to someone must have been unusual. Does this indicate that the language was one similar to Welsh but different enough to be troubling? This would be an unusual difficulty, and might have come if the people of Annwfn spoke Cornish, Cumbric or Breton, languages still relatively close to Old Welsh in this period. On the other hand, the difficulties could have been purely technical (perhaps the watchman was far away) or their language could have been completely different. I shall return to this point later.

The final two lines of this verse are just repeating what we have heard already. 'Golud' normally means 'wealth' but some translators have suggested it means 'hinderance' in this instance.

5.

I do not deserve the small men, trailing their shields

They do not know who was created on what day

What time in the middle of the day Cwy was created

Who made [the one] that did not go to Doleu Defwy?

They do not know The Brindled Ox (strong its head ring)

Seven-score links in his collar

And when we went with Arthur (sad tribulation)

Except seven, none returned from Fandwy Fortress

Verse five begins a bardic "boast" which is a motif found most commonly in poetry assigned to Taliesin[8], where the author asks a number of questions about the natural and metaphysical world to show how much more knowledgeable he is than his audience. Although the full flow of questions does not begin until verse 6, the learned nature of the poet's boast is demonstrated by how many of his points we understand, let alone can explain ourselves today. As far as I can tell, these questions are supposed to be a tirade about monks. Monk's shields are trailing (they don't fight) and they aren't familiar with tools of agriculture like the 'penrwy' literally head-ring (this could be a reference to the head-yoke, used on oxen in Britain before the neck-yoke was discovered and long before the Normans introduced plough-horses.) This tirade is mirrored in another poem, 'Mabygreu Taliesin' where he begins the poem by challenging the monks to answer his questions. Haycock has suggested that Cwy should be read as a scribal error for 'Dwy' (Lord God), which would lend a bit more sense to that line, and make it the question of the "first cause" which has perplexed scientists and theologians alike. This would only leave the fourth line unexplained, for which I can offer no suggestions. The last two lines again form a refrain, and this name for the fortress, 'Fandwy' probably means either 'God's peak' or 'God's place'.

6.

I do not deserve small men, trailing their vigour

---

[8] For a discussion of this feature, and of the range of Taliesin's knowledge of medieval cosmography, see *Fiery Shapes*, p.83 by Mark Williams.

They don't know what day created the chieftain

What hour in the middle of the day the owner was made

What animal they keep, silver its head

When we went with Arthur, sad strife

Except seven, none returned from Ochren Fortress

Verse six continues the Taliesin-style boast and tirade against monks. Lines two and three seem a variation of line three of verse five above, while the last two lines make our refrain, in a slightly different form again. Koch and Carey make 'Ochren' the 'enclosed fortress' but I cannot find this word in the *Geiriadur Prifyscol Cymru*, and Coe and Young leave it as 'Ochren'. Since the rest of the verse is essentially recycled material, line four may refer to the ox, although they do not typically have silver heads. Alternatively, the highest status dog in Britain at the time was a variant of the modern Irish wolfhound, which does have a silver coloured head, although I am not sure what use monasteries would have had for a hunting dog. If the poet knew that dogs were domesticated wolves, this might explain his boast that the monks do not know what animal they keep. Marged Haycock[9] suggests it may refer to the silver headed crozier which bore the reliquary box and was decorated with zoomorphic figures.

7.

Monks howl like a choir of puppies

[Shrinking] from an encounter of lords who know

Is there one course of wind? Is there one water of sea?

Is there one spark of fire (fierce tumult)?

Monks howl like wolves

[Shrinking] from an encounter of lords who know

---

[9] *Legendary Poems from the Book of Taliesin*, p.448

They do not know when dawn separates [from] midnight

Or of the wind: what is its course? What is its attack?

What place it destroys what land it strikes.

How many saints are lost, and how many alters?

I worship the Lord, Great Prince

May I not be sad, Christ provides for me.

Verse seven finishes the poem in great form, giving us several new questions demonstrating the poet's knowledge. While the poet asserts only that monks don't know the answer to his questions, the insinuation is that the poet does know all of the answers, and therefore his knowledge is far superior. The next line is even more confusing 'udyd ae gwydyanhawr' is an archaic phrase. 'Uddydd', (lords) is seen elsewhere, but the verb 'gwydyanu' is not attested elsewhere, Marged Haycock takes it as related to 'gwybod' (the ordinary verb 'to know') which is probably right. I shall return to the question of how he can know all of these things in the interpretation, but the poet's comparison between those who do and do not know is very interesting. Those who do not know are wolves or puppies. They make a lot of noise but they are not saying anything useful. The verb 'dychnut' used to describe them is confused. It can apparently both mean 'to howl' and 'to shirk', and it may have had both meanings here.

Interpretation

If we wanted to construct a Zecharia Sitchin style argument for Medieval Welsh literature, complete with references back to a race of space-travelling progenitors, this would be the text to use. Its language is very old, it is sceptical of monks and monastic learning and the lack of certain references to God outside of the last verse (which is different enough to suggest it could be interpolated) means that it could almost be directed at a non-Christian god. The name 'Cwy', if not a mistake for 'Dwy' (Lord God) could even provide an ancient name for one of these progenitors. Doubtless a similar sequence of letters and sounds could be found from other literary sources to support the theory that this poem preserves an ancient belief in exogenesis. Sadly however this simply is not admissible. Although there are certainly a number of old words like 'ri' which I mentioned earlier, and the plural suffix seen in 'bleidawr' is quite rare except early on, the general themes of magic, overt religion, and "the prisoner" and possibly "Taliesin's cauldron" motif suggest a late date for this text. There was no paganism in Welsh speaking Britain even in the ninth century, the oldest possible date for this text, and the church, although tolerant and even encouraging to Welsh vernacular culture at times, would not have accepted a multi-religion policy. Britain certainly provided its share of heresies, but these are all well (if sparsely) documented. Although it is true that Taliesin-style boasts like the one in verse seven show the effectiveness of a poet's training in medieval times, and suggest the writer thought himself better educated than monks, he does still believe in creation as shown in verse 5. But although it is easy to say what is not going on, it is harder to say quite what *is* happening.

I said in the introduction to this poem that we should view it as fiction set in the heroic age, rather than a factual account written in the past. On this basis we must therefore not look to this poem for description of an event, but rather as a source of motifs and topoi. Those which are strange, perhaps particularly those which are not often repeated elsewhere, deserve further consideration and we must question how the motif might have been conceived by the poet.

The motif of a fortress in the sea, which forms a gateway to Annwfn is one such motif. The appearance of this motif, fully formed, in a literature which does not have (as far as we know) any history of a sea-journey genre is highly suspect to my mind. It is true that neighbouring Ireland does have such a genre, but the details of the motif in 'Preiddeu Annwfn' are very different to those in any of the extant *navigatio* or *immram* stories from Ireland. Variants of this particular story may also have been known quite early-on. In *Historia Brittonum* (written 828-30, although we only have versions from the eleventh century) a similar story is told when describing the origins of the men of Ireland:

§13. And there they saw a tower of glass in the middle of the sea and they saw men on the tower and they tried to speak to them. They never replied, and in that same year they hastened to attack the tower with all their ships and with all women except [those in] one ship, which was broken by shipwreck, in that there were thirty men and the same number of women. And the other ships sailed to assault the tower, and once all had descended on the shore that was around the tower, the sea enveloped them and they were immersed and not one of them escaped.

The text goes on to explain that the one crew that was shipwrecked went on to repopulate Ireland. There are definite similarities between the events in 'Preiddeu Annwfn' and the events described above. Predominantly, in both a tower is accessible by sea (the fort in 'Preiddeu Annwfn' may well be an island, and the contended term 'Caer Wydyr' may be describing the fortress and refer to a tower of glass, if it does not refer to Glastonbury). In both cases there is some difficulty speaking with the inhabitants of the tower, and in both cases very few return, although the numbers differ. There are also differences. In 'Preiddeu Annwfn' the fortress seems to be a gateway to dark Annwfn, there are many people present, the fortress is not necessarily made of glass, and there is no indication that the sea swallows them. However, these are well within poetic license.

Having traced this motif, could it have had a basis in fact? Taking the points of agreement, these two texts refer to a tower (possibly made of glass) in the middle of the sea which easily destroys a host of men. The passage above suggests that the tower could either raise the levels of water around it, or, more probably, submerge its 'litore' (beach/shore). 'Preiddeu Annwfn' insists that this fortress was the gateway to Annwfn the underground otherworld. Could all this be describing a very large submarine? Such a vessel could have repelled an invasion with ease by submerging, and in the modern-day some deep-sea submarines, like the *Triton 36,000*, have been made from borosilicate glass, used because of its resistance to temperature chances and to the high pressure of the ocean's floor. This last vessel is designed to be capable of diving to the very deepest point on the earth (Challenger Deep), and carry two passengers with only limited experience with submarines. Of course the tower would need to be far bigger than this, but such a craft may be possible, especially if it does not need to go as low as the Triton 36,000.

The Triton 36,000.

Regardless of whether this structure is supposed to be a submarine or not, it seems clear that the occupants had a plan in place even as they completely ignored the Irish sailors in the episode I quoted above. Perhaps the crew of the submarine is not interested in interacting with the natives, since they make interaction hard for Arthur's retinue in the original text too. In both cases they are probably responsible for killing the majority of the crew which certainly does not inspire confidence in them.

If this was the last we heard of Annwfn the alien hypothesis would have very little worth, but the motif is seen again and again in Welsh and Irish legends. Take for example the second motif found in 'Preiddeu Annwfn', the strange artefacts: the 'peir pen annwfyn' (cauldron of the Head of Annwfn) and 'cledyf Lluch Lleawch 'Lightning's Slaughter sword'[10]. These two artefacts both seem to be from Annwfn. These are also both reminiscent of other artefacts found in Welsh literature which I discuss this point in "Cases of Powerful Artefacts". The Head of Annwfn is also a title given elsewhere in explanations of Annwfn, as for example in "The Case of Arawn of Annwfn" following.

Finally, I should make a note about how the poet might know all he claims to know. An expression preserved in the opening lines of Canu Llywarch Hen might help: 'Atwen ar fy awen' (I know on my awen). The 'awen' was the poetic inspiration of a poet. With it he could know anything. In the Irish poetic tradition bards were also able to prophecy the future with their inspiration, and this may have been the case in the Welsh tradition as well, since the greatest poets like Taliesin, Myrddin Wyllt and Aneirin were popularly assigned any prophetic texts. For the case of 'Preiddeu Annwfn' this is significant because I believe it is the central difference between the monks howling like wolves, and the 'lords who know'. The verb 'gwydyanu' is, as I said before, unattested elsewhere in Welsh literature but appears to be of common stock with the name 'Gwydion' who was a great magician in 'the Mabinogi', a quartet of legends set in the Welsh heroic age. Marged Haycock therefore suggests that this particular verb for knowing might refer to knowing by magic. I would argue that it probably means something that is known by poetic inspiration. Of course, one poem attributed to Taliesin (Angar Kyfundawt) claims that Awen is of Annwfn (the underworld), but this is probably just posturing, as the prophecies from medieval Britain are no more reliable than the prophecies from the rest of the world.

---

[10] Llwch (old Welsh Lluch) generally tends to refer to lightning, but it may have also been the name of a mythological figure related to Lug Lamfada of the Old Irish mythological cycle. See the Interpretation of the piece in "Cases of Powerful Artefacts"

The Case of Arawn of Annwfn

Introduction

The most famous story set in Annwfn in medival Welsh literature is probably the episode which occurs at the beginning of 'Pwyll'. 'Pwyll' is the first of the 'Four Branches of the Mabinogi', which are the traditional stories that make up the mainstay of Middle Welsh literature. These stories are prose tales with very occasional pieces of rhyme interspaced within them. They are completely traditional in nature, and their characters are not seen in other languages' medieval literature.

The 'Four Branches of the Mabinogi' (usually called in modern translations "The Mabinogion") are found in two main early manuscripts, the White Book of Rhydderch and the Red Book of Hergest. The White Book is the earlier of the two, most recently dated to around 1350, while the Red Book is dated to after 1382[11]. The relationship of these two versions to each other is still contended. Generally the Red Book is not thought to be a direct copy of the White Book but they are very close to each other to the extent that only a few words are different or in a different order between them. Extracts of other stories of the 'Mabinogi' have been found in Peniarth 6, a manuscript from the mid-thirteenth century, and although this does not include any part of 'Pwyll', Pwyll was probably also around by this stage. Actually, the language evidence of the 'Mabinogi' supports this theory, and suggests that stories were first written down in something very like their current form between the eleventh and twelfth centuries.

Certainly the language of the stories is older than those texts which were written in the fourteenth century like Marwnat Ithel ap Robert which we will come to later. However, because the language is prose rather than poetry, and prose written in a long prose tradition, the translation will probably seem "more modern" to readers. Considering only the age of the text, this impression is deceptive, as the text seems typical of the 'Mabinogi', with only a few older features in the first couple of text extracts. However, in terms of how deeply-set within the

---

[11] See: Daniel Huws, *Medieval Welsh Manuscripts*, p.82; 228 for the arguments.

text the topoi which we want to examine are, this story can be considered to be very much more polished and "further from the fact of the matter". The majority of the themes of the text can be discounted as purely literary fictions, and although I believe that a couple of the topoi of this story are relevant to us, they will be hard to tease out, as we shall see in the "Interpretation" section.

In this episode there are three main characters. Arawn is the king of Annwfn, which at this late stage in the literature is simply described a land bordering Dyfed, and neither underground nor across seas. Annwfn is an idyllic world, probably set fairly closely on paradisiacal fantasies of the writers and editors in the twelfth century. Unfortunately Arawn's kingship over Annwfn is not unchallenged, and Hafgen, another lord in Annwfn, over whose lands Arawn has no authority, is vying with him for control. Enter Pwyll, the Lord of Dyfed, a historic kingdom in the south-east of Wales. He wishes to earn Arawn's friendship.

The standard edition of this text is *Pwyll Pendeuic Dyuet* by R.L. Thomson, but this is out of print, and Ifor Williams' *Pedeir Keinc y Mabinogi* is still acceptable, and very much easier to get hold of since it is in the public domain in some countries. A translation of this story can be found at the beginning of any modern English version of *The Mabinogion* of which Lady Charlotte Guest's version is in the public domain and widely available online, although that particular translation leaves out the bedroom scenes of this story.

The Text

1.

A rider came after the pack [of hounds] atop a great, dapple-grey horse with a hunting horn around his neck, and wearing brown-grey cloth about him as [his] hunting clothes.

...

'Chief,' he [Pwyll] said, 'Good day to you, and what land do you come from, for your part?'

'From Annwfn,' said he, 'I am Arawn king of Annwfn.'

'Lord,' he said, 'What is the way that I will get your friendship?'

'Like this you may get it,' said he, 'There is a man who borders his territory with my own territory [who is] warring against me constantly. This is he: Hafgen, a lord from Annwfn. And by ridding me from oppression (and that you may do easily) you will get my friendship'

'For myself, I would do that,' he said, 'happily. [Just] you tell me *how* I may do it.'

'I will tell you' said he, 'Here is what you may do; I shall make a strong companionship with you. This is what I will do, I will put you in my place in Annwfn, and I will give the fairest woman you've ever seen to sleep with you each night, and [I will put] my own appearance and nature upon you, so that neither chamber-lad nor officer, nor [any] other man of those who has ever served me may notice that you are not me. And that' said he '[from] tomorrow until the end of the year from the day. Then we will meet in this place.'

'Well,' he said, 'Although I may be there until the end of the year, what guidance will be for me to catch the man that you tell of.'

'A year,' said he, 'from today, there is a meeting between he and I on the ford, and be in my shape there,' said he, 'and strike a single blow against him, he will not survive that. And although he may ask of you to give a second, do not strike, however he pleads with you! [Since] however I used to strike against him, he fought as well as before the next day moreover.'

Well,' he said, 'what shall I do with my domain?'

'I shall arrange it,' said Arawn himself, 'so there might not be in your realm either man or woman that notices that I am not you. And I shall go in your place.'

'Happily,' Pwyll said, 'and I myself shall go forth.'

'Your journey shall be unimpeded and no-one will trouble you, until you get to my domain, and I shall be leading you.'

He led him until he saw the court and the abode.

'Behold,' said he, 'the court and the domain in your power. And make for the court. There is not there anyone who will not recognise you, and as you watch the service there, you will understand the ways of the court.'

Part one describes the first meeting of Pwyll, the hero of our story, with Arawn, king of Annwfn. Because this particular story is so very long I have skipped a large chunk of the story after the first paragraph (I dislike doing this, since it takes the story a little out of its context ,but in this case the missing part is not relevant to us). It describes how Pwyll is out hunting. He spots a stag in the woods and chases it, but another set of hounds kill the stag before he can get there. These are peculiar in colour, they are shining white with red ears, which is a colour generally associated with otherworldly animals. He chases off the other hounds, and sets his own on the deer. The legality of this under the Welsh Laws of Court is a bit controversial – he might have been entitled to do it if we assume that he is in his own territory, and the hounds are those of one of his subjects. However, as we later hear, Arawn outranks him – he is a crowned king while Pwyll is only Lord of Dyfed (south-west wales). This probably means that he broke the law by pulling off Arawn's hounds, and therefore he is in trouble unless he can gain Arawn's friendship. This explains why Pwyll is so eager to do what Arawn bids him to do.

After the story is set up, Arawn asks Pwyll to impersonate him in his court for a year, and then, most importantly, kill his opponent in battle. The single combat seems to me to be the centre of this whole narrative, and it is very interesting that Arawn knows that Pwyll will be able to overcome his opponent easily, and insists that Pwyll should only strike twice. As I said at the beginning it is a common theme in many of the strange events and stories we are discussing that the strange characters appear as normal humans, but the ability to take on a different appearance is also common to normal mortal heroes in Welsh literature, so we probably should not take it as a preserved piece of knowledge about aliens.

2.

He himself made for court. And in the court he saw dormitories and halls and chambers and the most fair, beautiful buildings that anyone has seen. And he took to the hall to take off his boots. Squires and young lads came to take off his boots, and everyone greeted him well and knew him as they arrived. Two knights came to take his hunting cloth from around him and to dress gold-clothes of brocaded silk about him. And the hall was prepared.

Behold he saw a retinue and host, and the most handsome
and best-equipped host which anyone has seen [was]
coming inside. And the lady together with them, the fairest
woman that anyone has seen, and gold-clothes around her
of bright brocaded silk. And with that, they went to wash,
and they rose to tables, and they sat like this — the lady on
the one side of him, and the earl, he supposed, on the other
side. And a conversation started, between him and the
lady. And of all he ever saw, from conversations with her,
[he thought her] the noblest and the best-bred woman
[by] her nature and her conversation. And they spent time
eating and drinking, and enjoying music and carousing. Of
all the courts he'd seen of the Earth, here [was] the court
most abundant in food and drink, and gold plates and
princely jewels. Time came for them to go to sleep, and to
sleep they went, he and the lady. They went into bed
together [but] he turned his face to the bedside, with his
back to her. From then until the morning, he did not say
one word to her. The next morning, there was tenderness
and amiable conversation between them. Whatever
affection lasted between them through the day, there was
not one night until the end of the year that was different
from the first night.

This is a fairly typical Celtic otherworldly description, with everything described in its ideal form. Some of these things might happen individually in the world like knights and squires taking off a lord's shoes, a host looking very well ordered and the richest court he could imagine, but they would be unlikely to all correspond at once. Unfortunately again, because this motif is so common, it is unlikely to preserve any special knowledge of aliens. Similar descriptions of, for example, beautiful women are very common throughout Celtic literature.

Pwyll's refusal to sleep with the woman is certainly not through any prudishness on the parts of the scribes or storytellers, as forthcoming semgents will attest. It seems likely that it was placed in the story purely to propel the storyline of Pwyll and Arawn's friendship and is therefore probably not significant to us.

3

He spent the year through hunting and enjoying music, and carousing and making friends, and conversation with companions, until the night that [was] the date of the encounter. The date of that night came as well to the memory of the people of the extremities of the whole country [as to he himself]. And he, for his part, came to the appointment, and the gentlemen of the country together with him. And as soon as he got to the ford, a knight rose up and spoke like this:

'Gentlemen,' he said, 'hear-ye well, this appointment is [is] between the two lords, and that between the two persons alone. And each one of them is a claimant on the other, and that for the land and ground. And stay yourselves and leave it between them alone!'

And with that, the two lords closed together to the middle of the ford for an encounter. And on the first blow, the man that was in the place of Arawn struck Hafgan in the encounter in the centre of the boss of his shield so that it split into two halves, and all his armour broke, and so that Hafgan was [thrown the distance] of his arms and his spears over the crupper of his horse to the floor, with a mortal wound on him.

'Lord' said Hafgan, 'what right was yours to my death? I was not claiming anything from you. I don't know what cause you had for slaying me either. And by God' he said, 'since you have started my slaying, finish!'

'Ah Lord,' said he, 'It may yet be to my regret, accomplishing what I did to you. Find [another] who would slay you, I shall not kill you.'

'My loyal gentlemen,' he said, said Hafgan, 'bear me yonder; my death is determined. It is not proper for me to support you further.'

In extract three, what starts off as a very normal duel between the two, soon becomes very interesting. As was hinted earlier, Pwyll has absolutely no trouble defeating Arawn's opponent, and it only takes one blow. The last three paragraphs are perhaps the most intriguing. Hafgan appears to recognise immediately, from the way Pwyll struck him, that Pwyll is not Arawn, but another in his shape. It was clearly stated that Arawn was a claimant against Pwyll (he seems to be claiming his half of the realm), therefore only Arawn has the right to fight in the single combat against Hafgan. Hafgan is therefore rightfully upset with Pwyll for interfering.

The way by which Hafgan can tell that Pwyll is not Arawn was suggested earlier. Arawn, king of Annwfn told Pwyll that the fight would be easy for him, but that however many blows he, Arawn, had struck upon Hafgan, Hafgan had never taken any injury for longer than a single night. I would suggest that such a marked difference would be immediately obvious to Hafgan in the fight, even from just one blow This suggests that there is something special about Pwyll or his weapons or way of fighting which acts like kryptonite against inhabitants of Annwfn. However, the kryptonite effect seems to only work when only one blow is struck. Arawn cautioned Pwyll about this earlier, and Hafgan seems to be trying to trick Pwyll into striking him again in this extract. It is only after Pwyll refuses to strike him a second time that Hafgan exclaims 'neut teruynedic angheu y mi' (my death is determined). I shall discuss these theories in greater depth in the Interpretation.

The word for gentlemen in the last paragraph is "gwyrda" (lit: good-men). It is the same word that we find used in "The Case of Marwnad Ithel ap Robert" for the strange beings there. In this context it appears to designate the nobles of court and chief advisors (perhaps those that are called the 'uchelwyr' (high/noble-men) in the medieval Welsh law codes. It is important to note that the term is used in normal circumstances too, and we see it for example in part six of the current story as well, where it is clearly referring to normal noblemen who are not from the otherworld.

4

'My own gentlemen' said the man that was in the place of Arawn, 'take your accounts, and tell [me] which of the men should pay [allegiance] to me.'

'Lord,' said the gentlemen, 'all should pay it, since there is [no] king over all Annwfn except you.'

'Well' he said, '[for those] that come peacefully, justice shall be had. And [for those] that may not come obediently, they shall be forced by power of my arms.'

And with that, he took homage from the men and started to conquer their land. And by midday the next day, he was in possession of both lands.

And with that he set off along to his meeting-place, and he came to Glyn Cuch. And when he came there, there was Arawn, king of Annwfn meeting him. Each was happy to [see] the other of them.

'Well,' Arawn said, 'God repay you your companionship, I have heard of it.'

'Well,' said he, 'when you may come yourself to your country, you shall see all that I have done for your sake.'

'That which you have done,' he said, 'for my sake, may God reward you for it.'

Part four confirms the reason Arawn and Hafgan were fighting. They seemed to be contending for the rule of the whole of Annwfn, and now Hafgan is slain, Annwfn is united under one ruler. Whether this represents a civil war, the fight of two brothers, or whether Hafgan is merely using Pwyll to cease his fellow lord's kingdom is hard to tell, and is the sort of detail that would be easily changed from version to version of the story anyway. After subduing Hafgan's land, he goes to his rendezvous with Arawn as they arranged a year before. By the time he reaches Glyn Cuch (perhaps "Glen of Frowning") Arawn seems to already have heard of all that has occurred that day. Perhaps he was present in an earlier version of the story, or perhaps we are merely meant to take this at face value. Finally, there is perhaps a faint foreshadowing in the last thing Pwyll says to Arawn. Does this suggest that Pwyll knows Arawn will be pleased to hear that he did not sleep with Arawn's wife, even though part of what the king offered him originally was 'the fairest woman you've ever seen to sleep with you each night'?

5

5.

Then Arawn took his semblance, and returned to Pwyll,
Lord of Dyfed, his own. And he took to himself his own
form and returned to it. And Arawn journeyed forth
towards his court of Annwfn, and it was pleasant for him
to see with his host and with his retinue, since he had [last]
seen them a year ago. They however were had not missed
him, and his arrival was no different for them than before.
That day he passed through pleasure and happiness, and
sitting and conversation with his wife and with his
gentlemen. And when it was timelier to take sleep than
carouse, to sleep they went. Thus he went and his wife
went to him. At first he made conversation with his wife,
and [then] playing together with pleasurable passion and
love for her. And she had not been used to that for a year,
and she thought about that:

'Woe to God,' she said, 'What difference of thoughts has he
tonight compared with those of the year [before] tonight?'

And she thought long. And after she thought that, he
awoke, and he spoke a phrase and he spoke to her, and a
second time, and a third, and he did not get an answer
from her throughout that.

'What's the reason,' said he, 'that you don't speak to me?'

'I tell you' she said, 'I have not said for a year anything like as much as this'

'How come?' said he. 'We've always conversed.'

'Shame on me,' she said 'if there was [anything] between us the year before tonight from the time we would go between the bed clothes, we have not taken pleasure, nor conversed, nor have you turned your face to me — not to mention more than that!'

And then he thought, 'Oh Lord God,' said he, 'Strong and unique the friendship and ['tis] a loyal man I have received as a companion!'

And then he said to his wife: 'Lady' said he, 'don't blame me! Between myself and God,' said he 'I have not slept with you for the year before tonight, and I have not lain [with you]'

And then he told the whole tale to her.

'To God I swear my confession,' she said, 'a strong hold you have had on [your] companion since he fought with temptation of the body, and stayed loyal to you yourself!'

'Lady,' said he, 'that is the same thought I myself had, while I was silent to you.'

'That's not surprising!' she said.

Part five starts off quite interestingly. The way it describes the magic of appearance-changing suggests that a person has 'furyf e hun' (his own form) and that any form he puts on himself which is not his own is only ever a disguise, to be later cast off. However, elsewhere in the 'Mabinogi' animal shape-changers are sometimes said to have taken on the 'anyan' (nature) of the animals they turn into, so it may be that this is not always true.

The entirety of the remainder of this passage is made up of the crowd-pleasing realisation of how faithful Pwyll has been to Arawn by not sleeping with his wife. However, in my opinion this is probably part of the later trappings of the story and not part of the remembered-history we are interested in. If we want to extract the truth we have to first excavate the narratorial presence from the story, and without an omniscient narrator, the audience of this story could have had no idea what was said in a private bedroom.

6.

He himself, Pwyll, Lord of Dyfed, went to [his] domain and his land. And he started interviewing the land's gentlemen, [asking] how he had been as lord over them the length of that year [compared] to [how] he had been before that.

'Lord,' they said, 'your honour has not been as good; you yourself have not been such a kind young man, it has not previously been so easy for you to share your wealth, your rule has never been better than this year!'

'Between myself and God,' he said, 'This is the proper thing for you, to thank the man that was with you, and here is the tale [just] like it was' — and Pwyll told them all.

'Well Lord,' they said, 'thanks to God you got that companionship; and the lordship we have had that last year, you won't take it from us, we know!'

'I shall not, between myself and God!' Pwyll himself said.

And from then onwards, a very strong companionship stated between them, and each one of the companions sent horses and greyhounds and hawks and all such jewels, if he thought each one would please the thoughts of his companion. And because he spent that year in Annwfn, and ruled over there successfully, and he brought the two kingdoms into one through his very valiant nature and his warfare, a name is given to Pwyll, Lord of Dyfed, and he was called "Pwyll, Head of Annwfn' from then onwards.

Part six starts out in exactly the same way as part five, with Pwyll talking to his own 'gentlemen', and finding that his realm has prospered under the guardianship of Arawn. This is clearly also a feature designed to engender friendship between Arawn and Pwyll, and friendship does indeed come in the last paragraph. This last paragraph is however, very relevant for its own sake. The gifts I will consider in more detail later on, but the title is very important. 'Pen Annwn' (Head of Annwfn) is the same title given in "The Case of Preiddeu Annwfn" for the cauldron (or perhaps the owner of the cauldron). Unlike 'gwyrda' (gentlemen) which we discussed above, 'Pen' is a less normal title. It has a similar semantic range of meanings as the English 'head' (it is the normal word for the body part, and the top of something) but can also be used for "at the end of". It is at least understandable as 'leader' here, and common in suffixed forms like 'penadur'. However, 'pen annwn' seems very much like a set title rather than a generic one.

Interpretation

As I said at the introduction to this episode, if there is any truth hidden in this story, it is very deep down. The story as I have translated it is a highly polished medieval drama, and we would be remiss to believe that any of the events in it happened exactly as they are described here. On the other hand, I do believe that fiction can be useful for our purposes, so long as we are looking at topoi and motifs rather than trying to take fictional stories literally.

I will not consider all of the interesting features which I pointed out during the translation of this text. Many of them were interesting only in the context of the translation, whilst some of them are interesting but may have entirely innocent explanations. For example, the appearance of white, red eared hounds is certainly a common motif for otherworldly animals, but the motif may simply reflect that some leucistic and albino creatures, as for example the herds of white, red-eared cattle known to have existed in Britain not so long ago, were of very high status. As we have seen, the otherworld is full of the best of everything, so naturally all their animals would be of the highest grades.

However, what I have called the "central topos" of this story, that is, the duel between Hafgan and Pwyll, which establishes Arawn as the king of all Annwfn is of central importance. Our interest in this topos can be broken down into four questions: (i) What was Hafgan's "kryptonite", which meant Pwyll could slay him so easily, when Arawn could not? (ii) Why was it so important that Pwyll only struck Hafgan once? (iii) How did Hafgan recognise Pwyll? and (iv) Why were Arawn and Hafgan fighting in the first place?

To start with the last question, Arawn and Hafgan were each clearly described as a 'hawlwr' (legal claimant) (§3), meaning that they were contending about who was the rightful owner of land. Duels seem to have been an acceptable way to settle legal disputes under medieval Welsh law (before English law was enforced), so this would probably have been very understandable for a medieval audience.

In extract one, Arawn describes Hafgan as 'warring against him constantly' and his realm as 'bordering on mine'. This strongly suggests that, although Arawn considers himself the crowned king of Annwfn, he is not sovereign over Hafgan's realm. Therefore it is clear that, to answer (iv), each of the two claimants wanted to take over the other's territory, which is what happened at the end when Pwyll finally persevered in the single combat.

Also in extract one, Arawn made it clear that Pwyll would find it easy to beat Hafgan. Indeed, when it comes to the fight, it is clear that this is the case. With a single blow from Pwyll, Hafgan is thrown a couple of metres from his horse, his shield shatters, his armour shatters and he acquires a deadly wound. This is partly due to the style of Welsh battle descriptions, which do often describe heroes as easily overcoming their adversaries in one way fights. However, I believe that something more than this is indicated by the description. Pwyll does not seem to be an especially mighty fighter, nor is Hafgan a stranger to combat. From Arawn's explanation we know that the two of them used to spend days raining blows upon each other. And yet it seems that Hafgan has no defence from Pwyll's single blow. This suggests that something about Pwyll is radically different to those around him. If it was just a matter of his sword, or his armour, it seems to me that Arawn would have been able to overcome Hafgan himself. He certainly knew about Hafgan's weakness. That he was unable to overcome Hafgan himself suggests that whatever Hafgan's weakness, he is unable to take advantage of it, perhaps because he suffers from the same weakness himself.

If it is possible that this topos was originally based on descriptions of a fight between aliens and humans, then the weakness could be anything from sheer physical weakness – perhaps the aliens of Annwfn could be simply a frailer species despite closely resembling humans? Or perhaps their tactics and weapons are so different that the original entity seeking help (the Arawn figure) had no hope of using one against his rival (the Hafgan figure)? Or finally, perhaps the Hafgan figute was expecting another kind of fight, one with psychic abilities to which humans are not susceptible. Sadly, as I have said, to answer (i), the topos is very deeply embedded within this story now, and we can only speculate about the nature of the weakness. It is very similar to the weakness shown in the "Case of the Coranieid", in which another species perfectly resembling humans demonstrates a weakness.

Whatever the answer to question (i) it probably suggests an answer to question (ii). From Arawn's insistence that Pwyll should not strike more than once in part one, to Hafgan apparently trying to trick him into striking again in part three it seems clear that Hafgan has some way of nullifying the power of any blows he is struck by more than once. Again, if we take this topos as containing a memory of an alien's abilities, it seems to describe some way of learning about ways of fighting, which require the learner to be struck twice. To answer (ii) then, apparently, once the learner (or Hafgan in this case) is struck twice they then know enough about the blows to undo all of their effects. Perhaps in fact this was Hafgan's kryptonite (the answer to (i)) – because Arawn had struck him Hafgan than once, after this he was unable to ever kill him with a blow.

This also answers (iii). Because, whether because he was unlike all the other inhabitants of Annwfn, or because he had never struck Hafgan before, Pwyll was able to strike a terrible blow to Hafgan, he was immediately recognisable as *not* Arawn, who was unable to do any damage to Hafgan.

This is probably the episode in this book which is the most speculative, and which requires the most interpretation to remove from its context. It may well be that even if I have persuaded you that there is some strange basis to this legend, you are not convinced of my interpretation of which parts of the text are medieval trappings, and which form the kernel of the legend. However, before we finish I should make a few more points.

First, regarding the title 'pen annwn' (Head of Annwfn) which is given to Pwyll. As I explained in my commentary on part six, this is a strange title, and sounds like a set epithet given to chieftains of Annwfn. It also comes up in "The Case of Preiddeu Annwfn" (extract two).

The reference to the exchange of gifts between Arawn and Pwyll at the end of the story may also be based on reality. As explained in "Cases of Powerful Artefacts", many of the more peculiar and "magical" items in medieval Welsh literature are described as from Annwfn. Doubtless this became an easy way to explain items used as plot devices, but it is quite conceivable that some of the earliest powerful artefacts may have been given by, stolen from or salvaged from alien predecessors. Such artefacts need not have been technological marvels. Before the advent of the blast furnace in Britain in the middle medieval period, steel would have been relatively rare, and artefacts made of these, or even stronger materials might have been rightfully considered as quite marvellous. See "Cases of Powerful Artefacts" for more on this theme.

There is also one later quote in the 'Mabinogi' which suggests that this topos was quite an original part of the story. In 'Math' which is the fourth branch, an early part of the plot is based around some creatures which have been introduced into Wales from Annwfn:

'Lord,' said Gwydion, 'I have heard [of] a type of creature [that] has never come to this island [before] coming to the south.'

'What is their name' said he [Math].

'Hogs, Lord.'

'What kind of animals are these ones?'

'Small animals, their meat is better than beef. They are small; and changing names. "Pigs" they are called now.'

'To whom do they belong?'

'Pryderi, son of Pwyll, sent to him from Annwfn by Arawn, King of Annwn.'

After Gwydion has described them, he goes to Dyfed to steal the bacon producers away from Pryderi, the son of Pwyll who was the hero in the text we just discussed. The only problem with this quotation is that wild boar are native to Britain, and in the medieval period, our bristling, tusked domestic pigs were not significantly different from the wild creatures. Therefore any claim that these creatures were recently introduced must be fictional. How should we interpret this passage then? Firstly, although wild boar do not seem to become completely extinct in Britain until the seventeenth century, there is some suggestion that these creatures were becoming rare by the thirteenth century[12], and were only kept as as novelties after this. This might explain how an author in the twelfth or thirteenth century could become confused about where pigs came from. Additionally, wild boar may well have been re-introduced to the writers area to create a hunting ground.

Secondly, much of the other livestock in early medieval Britain (cows, horses, sheep, goats) seem to have been brought over in either the Neolithic or Bronze Age to facilitate the hunting of these creatures. It remains a contended issue whether medieval "domestic" pigs were brought to Britain as well, like they were to the rest of Europe, but domestic pigs and wild boar can be distinguished in the archaeological record by the size of their teeth, which may indicate some difference in stock. I cannot accept the idea that any part of the 'Mabinogi' was formed even in the Bronze Age, but, if we can accept one introduction of the species to an area then we can accept more than one. Despite sheep being present for more than 5000 years in Britain, additional, better stocks sheep were imported by the Romans and also the Danes. Perhaps the same is true of pigs. If there was originally a story that a better stock of pig was introduced, and then wild boar became rare, later writers and editors might misunderstand the story, and assume that it referred to the original introduction of the species. In that case this story could be true. It need hardly be pointed out that any alien species sufficiently technologically advanced to get here could probably either genetically enhance our stock of domestic meat, or ferry over creatures from far lands which had been selectively bred. However, at

[12] See Derek Yalden, *The History of British Mammals*, p.98;168, for a summary of the archaeological evidence)

present there is no archaeological evidence for any sudden significant change in pig stock in Britain, meaning that this is currently only speculation.

The Case of the Coranieid

Introduction

If 'Pwyll', the story we looked at above is one of the most influential and important prose stories in Welsh literature, perhaps one of the least well known is 'Cyfranc Lludd a Llefelys' (The account of Lludd and Llefelys). Although this story is found modern translations of *The Mabinogion* it is not one of the historic 'Four Branches of the Mabinogi'. It is however found in the same early manuscripts of the 'Mabinogi', that is, The Red Book of Hergest and The White Book or Rhydderch, which both date to the second half of the fourteenth century, and which I discussed in the Introduction to "The Case of Arawn of Annwfn". This means that although the standard edition is *Cyfranc Lludd a Llefelys* by Brynley Roberts, the story is well translated in almost every English version of *The Mabinogion.* For the purposes of this text, Lady Charlotte Guest's edition is now in the public domain, and so is available for free online, and so my translation can be checked against hers quite easily.

Uniquely among the stories associated with *the Mabinogion* however, this story is also told in 'Brut y Brenhinedd' which is a Welsh version of 'Historia Regum Brittaniae' (The History of the Kings of Britain), a Latin text by Geoffrey of Monmouth. In 'Historia Regum Britanniae', Geoffrey attempts to put all of the legends about Britain into one long history of the island. It is present in this form from the Llanstephan 1 manuscript (of the early thirteenth century) onwards. This is especially interesting because although Lludd is mentioned in the original version of 'Historia Regum Britanniae', his Welsh 'Cyfranc' is not told. Considering how thorough Geoffrey seems to have been at finding legends this has suggested to some[13] that the story was not written until after Geoffrey's work was completed around 1136. However the *argumentum e silencio* is not especially strong when we consider that none of the other stories associated with *the Mabinogion* are present in 'Historia Regum Britanniae' either. The language of 'Lludd a Llefelys' does however seem more modern than the language of the proper *Mabinogi*. It is also very influenced by Latin with long, drawn out sentences. In my translation I have tried to artificially split some of the longer of these in my

---

[13] See Brynley Roberts' edition of the text, p.xv.

translation, but they are still recognisable because all my artificial sentences start with words in square brackets.

The main plotline of 'Cyfranc Lludd a Llefelys' involves three 'gormes' (oppressions, plagues) which Lludd, the king of Britain wishes to rid the island of. The first of these is a scream, heard across Britain every May-day, which is eventually attributed to Britain's resident dragon, trying to protect Britain from another dragon (probably meant to represent the Saxons). This story is very similar to one found in the earlier original version of *Historia Regum Britanniae.* The second is the strange disappearance of food from Lludd's court. This story is very similar to one found in an Irish story called 'Macgnímartha Finn' and probably is more original to the Irish tradition than the Welsh. Finally, the third is the appearance of the Coranieid, a group of people with the power to hear anything said about them, even a whisper. This episode seems to be original to our text, and is the one that we will be examining here.

It is worth pointing out that the very name, Coranieid, suggests that these people are a completely separate nationality, different to the Brytanieid (native Britons/Welsh and Cornish), Romanieid (Romans) and 'Sayson' (Saxons). Various attempts to link this name with historically known groups on linguistic grounds have failed (see: Brynley Roberts standard edition, pp.xxxii-iii). Since only a small part of this story is relevant to us, I have again translated only a certain amount of the story, and I have left without translation a gap between extracts four and five. Although this means that my translation is not continuous, I have given notes about the parts I do not translate in the commentary and I believe that this story can be understood on its own with only a small amount of explanation.

The Text

> 1
>
> And after a length of time passed, three oppressions fell on the Island of Britain the like of which no-one had seen before. The first of them was [in] the form of a race that came that was called the Coranieid. So vast was their knowledge that there was no speech across the face of the island that was spoken so low [that when] the wind caught it they didn't hear of it, and because of that, harm could not be done to them.

Before our extract, this story starts off introducing Lludd, and Llefelys who are the sons of 'Beli Mawr', a character in Welsh mythology very often mentioned but who is never properly described. Lludd becomes king of Britain and founds London, and Llefelys becomes king of France.

'Gormes' in this context is traditionally translated 'plagues' but something like 'oppressions' or even 'scourges' also fits the meaning and possibly suits the context better. The way that this oppression is described is very interesting. It was the Coranieid's 'gwybod' (knowing/knowledge) which meant they could hear everything. This is very suggestive, but I shall leave my explanation for the Interpretation section.

Although the sense of "the form of a race" in English suggests that the Coranieid physically did not resemble the Britons, in Welsh this is a perfectly natural way of describing the oppression, and we later learn that they are physically indistinguishable from the Britons, a familiar story found in most of my Case files.

2

And from that King Lludd got a lot of stress and worry for himself, since he didn't know which way to take to rid himself from those oppressions. And he called to him all the gentlemen of the realm and asked counsel of them [regarding] what thing they should do against those oppressions. And from the general counsel of the gentlemen, Lludd son of Beli went to Llefelys his brother, king of France, because that man was a great one for counsel and wise, to take counsel with him. And then they made a fleet and those secretly and silently, lest that race know the reason for the errand, [they] or anyone [else] except the king and his councillors. And after they were ready, they went in their ships. Lludd and [those] that he chose [were] together with him, and he started cleaving the seas on the way to France. And after that news came to Llefelys, since he did not know the reason for the fleet of his brother, he himself came out to meet him with his ships, (huge was their number). And after Lludd saw that, he left all the ships and he met his brother. He himself came out in one ship and his brother came to meet [him], and after they came together, each one of them put both hands [on the] neck of his companion and from brotherly love each one welcomed his companion to him.

Not much happens in this extract, but I wanted to include it to stop extracts one and three from appearing out of context, and because it is a fairly succinct description. I should again reiterate at this point though, that this story is very definitely fictional. Although Lludd (sometimes called Llaw Ereint) is mentioned elsewhere, there are no other real stories about him, and there is no evidence that he ever really existed as the king of Britain, and the same goes for his brother Llefelys. Lludd's name is mentioned fairly early however, and there is even some fairly flimsy evidence that equates Lludd with a local god in Roman times. We shall consider this further in the Interpretation.

The Coranieid are not mentioned here by name, but they are almost certainly those implicated by "that race". A new fleet would involve the co-operation of many shipwrights, engineers, sailors, labourers and perhaps the medieval equivalent of canteen staff. This storyteller's idea, that a government could plausibly hide its secret solution from all of its subjects without any problems with secrecy, might find some resonance with readers today.

There are two particularly poetic turns of phrase in this extract: First, the concept of a ship 'rwygaw' (cleaving) the 'moroed' (seas) is not the normal way of describing navigation, and suggests a Latin, or perhaps Old English influence. Second, I believe the last sentence is deliberately meant to keep readers guessing. The whole of extract two builds up to that sentence, with Llefelys wandering if Lludd has come to make war and bringing his own imposing fleet, and then Lludd approaching that fleet on his own. If I am right, when each of the brothers 'aeth dwylaw mynwgyl y gilyd' (put hands [on the] neck of his companion, this made the original audience of the text believe they were about to choke each other, just as much as an English audience reading the translation. We can almost hear a dramatic pause before the audience is assured that the hands on the neck were as an embrace.

3

And after the reason for his errand was told by Lludd,

Llefelys said that he himself knew the reason he [Lludd]

had come to those lands. And thus they took council about [how] they could converse about their mission in a different [way] than [normal], so that the wind would not go around their speech, lest the Coranieid know that which they said. And then Llefelys arranged a long horn to be made from bronze and through that horn they conversed. However, what[ever] speech was said by one of them to the other through the corn, the other one of them did not get [anything except] quite hateful conversation back. And after Llefelys saw that, and [he knew] that there was a devil obstructing them and making trouble through the horn, he himself arranged wine to be poured into the horn and cleaned it, and through the power of the wine, the devil was driven from the horn.

Extract three seems rather peculiar from a modern perspective. It was explicitly said in extract two that Llefelys wasn't sure why Lludd was in his kingdom, and this caused all of the dramatic tension. Therefore how does Llefelys know now? It seems we are to understand that Lludd explained his three oppressions, and Llefelys understood that he wanted a cure for them without Lludd explicitly saying so. We then come to the strange horn. Is the 'kythreul' (devil/demon) somehow controlled by the Coranleid? If so how would they have known that a horn was being made? If not, why did the author include such an interpolation? It seems to me that either there is something about the devil which has not been explained, or it represents an element added later. Regardless, this extract provides a route whereby the two characters can talk privately. But nobles in this period would probably have been capable of writing messages to each other on wax tablets if not expensive parchment. Did the storyteller not consider this? These would all be relevant questions to ask of a storyteller in modern times, but perhaps we should not expect our modern ideas of the aesthetics of storytelling to exactly agree with those of the medieval period.

I should comment on one word before moving on. 'Rinnwed' properly refers to the attribute or ability of something, but it is almost always used to describe a mysterious or supernatural ability. In this context, by the mysterious power of the wine the devil was driven from the horn.

4

And after [that] their conversation was untroubled, Llefelys told to his brother [that] he would give to him a species of insect. [He should] leave some of them alive to breed for fear of the chance of a second coming of that kind of oppression, but take others of the insects and crush them in water and that, he confirmed, would be good at destroying the race of Coranieid. Thus, after he might come home to [his] kingdom, he should summon all the people together, his race and the race of the Coranieid into one assembly. [Then] pretending to make peace between them, when they were they were all of them together, take that powerful water and throw it over everyone at once, and, he confirmed, that water would poison the race of the Coranieid and neither kill nor harm his own race...

Extract four is the important one from our perspective. The most intriguing thing is obviously the idea that insects could save Britain from the Coranieid. Unfortunately the word for insect used (pruet) is just the medieval plural form of the modern Welsh word 'pryf' (insect, bug). In modern times the name usually refers to grubs and worms, but historically, looking at the various derivatives, it could probably refer to anything from grubs and worms to spiders, flies and small pest mammals. Lludd was told to 'briwaw' (bruise, mash, wound) these, which probably discounts only the small mammals. I shall discuss which insects could be responsible and how they could kill the Coranieid in the Interpretation.

Again there are what we would call modern plot holes in this story. Why did Llefelys just happen to have a colony of the exact insects required with him. How was Lludd to care for his insects? How could all the citizens of Britain fit anywhere, let alone find time to travel to see him? But discounting these plot-holes as merely indicative of the later trappings of the storyteller, we have a clear resolution in sight now.

5

...And then Lludd returned back to [his] country and without delay he summoned to him everyone in the whole of his race and of the Coranieid. And as Llefelys taught him, he crushed the insects in the water and threw that at once over everyone. And immediately he thus destroyed the whole nation of the Coranieid without harm to anyone among the Britons...

The gap between parts four and five consist of Llefelys suggesting answers for Lludd's other two oppressions (although he is not given any special stage-props for these). The deed is accomplished as easily as Llefelys suggested. Although to the modern imagination, the text suggests Lludd only crushed the insects after everyone had arrived, (perhaps whilst making a dramatic Hollywood style speech), the terse style of the text does not demand this explanation. We might rather assume he took a bit longer over it, perhaps crushing many bugs, although the mixture may not have stayed fresh for too long.

There is one final, but very important point I must make here. If the Coranieid were physically distinguishable from normal humans, there would be no point gathering everyone together. Humans could simply keep containers of anti-Coranieid liquid handy, and spray anything that looked different, much like modern people keep bug spray. You might say that he did this to keep the element of surprise, and for fear that there would be reprisals later if he did not surprise them. However, any species capable of reprisals would be unlikely, in my opinion, to answer the summons of a human king. I believe it most probable that the Coranieid were disguised, like all the other races under discussion in this book.

Interpretation

It is impossible to prove that this story is true, and, in fact, many details of the story in this form are indisputably inaccurate. There was probably never a man called Lludd, and if there was he was certainly never the King of Britain. No-one could summon all the people of Britain together at once, he probably did not get the insects from his brother in a high tension boat meeting. The devil in the horn episode probably has no basis in reality. Someone in that situation in real life would undoubtedly have considered writing, unless it took place before writing became common in Britain (pre-Roman times).

On the other hand, if we are looking for aliens in Welsh literature, this may perhaps be one of the best possibilities. We are hearing about a species defined by having so much knowledge it can hear everything caught by the wind. A modern person going into the past might be able to impersonate a member of this species quite easily. We have had electronic "bugs" and recorders, made to listen in to other people's conversations for quite some time. If they brought enough of these (with a suitable power supply) our modern person could quite soon get a reputation for hearing everything – or at least everything that mattered. The Coranieid also have some abilities which we do not at present. First, they seem to be also able to disguise themselves to create their "oppression" on Britain. Also, there is sufficient physiological difference between this race and the race of the Britons that a poison which kills one will not at all effect the second. Both of these factors strongly support the idea that this thread of the story could be discussing an alien invasion of sorts.

If we want to consider all of the possible alien appearances in Welsh literature, then we should proceed with the working theory that the latest form of the story is irrelevant and fictional but that the essential topos of the invading species was recycled from an older piece of factual oral history.

Unfortunately not much about the Coranieid is discussed. We don't know why their arrival was counted as a 'gormes' (oppression, plague), but we do know that the Britons wanted to get rid of them enough to try and fight them even though they could hear everything. It's probably safe to take their great knowledge as great technology, and their technology seems superior to ours, with bugs but also the ability to completely physically disguise themselves. We can tell however, that this appearance was only an illusion because they were affected by the bugs. Any bodies different enough to die from these bugs probably should be naturally at least subtly distinguishable from humans, but the Coranieid were not, as I have discussed, suggesting they were in disguise (but not in human bodies).

These Coranieid do not seem to be the same race as the people of Annwfn. As we have seen, these latter live on their own, and seem to dislike interactions with all but a chosen few. Likewise, they do not seem like the visiting 'Eingl' with their natural disasters and bright lights from 'The Case of Marwnad Ithel ap Robert'. Perhaps we are looking at a third species, although there is really very little material here to go on.

Ultimately this story is all about stopping an alien invasion, and all I have done so far is discuss whether these aliens are fictional or factual, and what their nature is. Perhaps instead, the really important question is how they were killed. It may be impossible to determine if the story is true or false, but either way the destruction may be worth focussing on. If false, it forms a fun medieval science fiction, if true, it may one day save the world once again! Interestingly, just like Hafgan of Annwfn, the Coranieid had their own brand of "kryptonite" which took the form of a mixture made of squashed bugs and water.

The most important question is obviously what kind of bugs Llefelys gave. Unfortunately there is not an easy answer to this. However, there are a few clues, if we can trust the fundamentals of the story as we have it. We are looking for an insect which when crushed either contains or produces a powerful chemical. Its body ought to only release this chemical when freshly killed, as Llefelys specifically gave Lludd a breeding collection, suggesting that the creatures are of no use when long dead. The deadly-substance is also one that should diffuse through water (i.e. probably a liquid, like most fresh insect-juice). Finally, since Llefelys gave Lludd the creatures, this suggests that they might not be "native" or common in Britain.

People in the medieval period had an amazing knowledge of the properties of animals and plants. Crushed insects and spider webs were staples of the apothecary and also of the scriptorium, where they made ink pigments. I am not a naturalist or a chemist or a physician, but my best guess as to the identity of the beetle concerned would be the 'shield bug', which is an insect similar to the 'stink bug' of America. In Britain the most common type is *Palomena Prasina* (the green shield bug) but there are various others. The reason these bugs are so well known is because they exude a very noxious odour when handled or touched. The chemical constituents of this odour vary depending on the type of shield bug, but many contain cyanide compounds. Although cyanide in many forms is horribly dangerous to humans, perhaps Llefelys found a form or dosage not dangerous to humans. One possible use relies on the fact that cyanide poisoning normally occurs when humans consume or breathe in the substance. As mammals, humans are fairly resistant to liquid poisoning through the skin unlike for example, amphibians. As long as none was allowed to enter the eye, and none of the humans had undressed wounds, they would be quite safe from a low exposure. Human clothing would also help resist the substance.

I also contacted an etymologist. Hania Berdys, the manager of the Garden Safari project (www.gardensafari.net). She suggested that the Dock Leaf Bug (Coreus Marginatus) fits the description. This is a variety of shield bug which produces copious amounts of a chemical that can dye human skin brown. However, Hania also pointed out that if we allow the Coranieid to have an existing genetic intolerance to certain chemicals a vast field of possibilities is opened up. Just like the way some humans are allergic to bees and wasps and can die from getting stung, other species' genetic intolerances could make them just as susceptible to any other insect.

Dock Leaf Bug (Coreus Marginatus). Picture © Hania
Berdys, www.gardensafari.net.

Dr. Florin Feneru, an Identification Officer at the Natural History
Museum tentatively suggested to me that one of the various species of
bombardier beetles may fit the description. From what I have been able
to find out these are more common in France than in Britain and their
bodies have a similar defence mechanism. They produce and store
hydrogen peroxide and hydroquinones. When the creature feels
threatened it presses these chemicals into a reacting chamber together.
The chemicals react exothermically and then the resultant mixture is
released at boiling hot temperatures which can kill insects. The mixture
is so corrosive it can even irritate human skin. Interestingly for our
circumstances however, hydrogen peroxide on its own (squeezed out of
the creature) may be the key. It can bleach human skin, but is usually
stored in water (like the vat in our story). At low concentrations (<3%) it
is of no danger to humans whatsoever, and is even used as an
ingredient in toothpaste. However when it comes into contact with
alcohols or hydrocarbons it can act as a contact explosive. At higher
concentrations (>50%) it is more corrosive, and can be especially
dangerous if allowed to enter the body through an eye, mouth or
undressed wound. However it decays on contact with sunlight and
therefore keeping the bugs might be the only way to keep a ready
supply of the chemical.

Ultimately if we are to accept the account about the Coranieid as having a kernel of truth, it doesn't especially matter which bugs were used. The important things to remember are that (i) alien species have different physiology to humans, regardless of their appearance (ii) they are probably more vulnerable to contact with water based chemicals than humans are, and this may suggest that their skin is not as developed as ours and (iii) they can be killed just like humans.

Lludd as a god

There is one final thing which still needs to be discussed concerning Lludd. There is a widespread belief that Lludd is a god. If I believed it, this would suit me perfectly. I could claim that he was a local hero, and the legends of him defeating the Coranieid made people consider him a god. I could even claim that he was an alien himself, who, in passing, released the Britons from the grasp of the Coranieid. This would lend a definite antiquity and even a certain prestige to my claims. Doubtless a writer with more ambition and less scruples would have no qualms milking this commonly believed factoid. However, I have said from the start that I wanted this book to have some integrity. *'Readers need make only the following allowances whilst reading – that aliens may exist, may have visited Britain, and may have been written about in the past'*. I will not deceive you about what the literature says, and I will not deceive you about what its words mean. The Interpretation sections are highly speculative, but they are led by the facts of each case, they do not inform the facts of each case. In exactly the same way, I don't want to deceive you about Lludd. He is certainly a real medieval character. Also, since the two other main storylines in 'Lludd a Llefelys' (the fighting dragons and the food-stealing magician) seem to be literary borrowings from elsewhere, it does seem likely to me that the story of the Coranieid was also an older borrowing rather than a thirteenth century invention. However, there is not sufficient evidence that he was ever a god. I believe that it is worth the time to explain why he cannot be a god, but it will form one of the most scholarly sections of the book. I have therefore consigned it to a separate chapter-part, and if you are not interested in the answer you are perfectly safe skipping to the next chapter from here.

The view of Lludd as a god depicts him as a character who has undergone 'euhemerisation'. This is a scholarly word designating the medieval process whereby pagan gods were sometimes demoted to heroes or local fairies upon contact with the Catholic Church. When this happened people could still tell stories about their gods, and even sometimes pray to them and worship them if they became saints. A popular example in the Celtic world is Saint Brigit (or Brìde to use the British (Scottish) form). Although now most known as a very popular saint, originally she seems to have been an important god in Ireland. It appears that when Ireland was Christianised, she was allowed to become a saint (complete with a history of her birth, and miracles she performed).

There is nowhere near the same level of evidence for Lludd as there is for Brigit. The evidence we have is mainly from a single verse found in the Black Book of Carmarthen. This manuscript was written around 1250, but is mostly made up of Welsh verse some of which may have been written up to two or three hundred years earlier. The verse is found as part of a dialogue between Gwyn ap Nudd and Gwydneu Garanhir (a character mentioned in one of the earliest Welsh texts, 'Y Gododdin'):

> My horse is Carngrun, horror of battle
>
> 'Tis I [who] am called Gwyn, son of Nud
>
> Lover of Creiddylad, daughter of Lludd[14]

To be fair this does give us a bit more information about Lludd. However, upon seeing this, the nineteenth century scholars started looking for more links. There is also a Romano-British god, whom we only know of from one site, Lydney Park. He is called Nodens based on the inscription evidence (there are four inscriptions referring to: M. Nodenti, Nudente, Nodonti and [No]dentis[15]). This character may have been a healer god, as all sorts of model metal body parts have been found there – it was a common practice in Roman times to buy and "offer" model body parts, representing your injured ones to healer gods and goddesses. He is also closely associated with dogs, and many statuettes and depictions of dogs were also found.

In Old Irish there is also a character called Nuada. Two irregular forms of this name are attested, 'Nodain' and 'Nodan'. Various suggestions have been given for similarities between the god and the hero, the most

---

[14] Jenny Rowland's *Early Welsh Saga Poetry* is the standard edition and translation of this text.

[15] See Tolkien's 'The Name Nodens' in Mortimer-Wheeler's 1932 excavation report of Lydney Park.

common (and ridiculous) of which is that Nuada is, at one point, given a silver arm to replace an arm lost in battle, which matches a votive arm found at Lydney[16]. The fact that a votive leg, and other parts were also found at Lydney is, unsurprisingly, rarely mentioned. However those irregular forms are fairly convincing by themselves, although they could be purely coincidental.

So far none of the links are too tenuous, but the biggest stretch comes with scholars attempts to link Nuada and Nodens with Nud, and ultimately Lludd. Not only are the names similar (so the argument goes) but, Lludd has a once attested strange name 'Lludd Llaw Ereint' (Lludd silver-handed). Because of Nuada's silver hand in the Irish material he was similarly called Nuada argatlam (Nuada silver-handed). Thus the suggestion was made that Nuada and Nodens are one, and that Nuada was called Nud east of the Irish sea, and that the first letter of his name was changed to an 'L' due to "alliterative assimilation" (i.e. to make the 'llaw ereint' bit, which is never used, sound better). All these links were made despite the fact that these characters share no stories in common (except Nudd and Lludd), and are not even alike in character. The only story they do share is the one above, which has made some suggest that Gwyn and Creiddylad should be seen as incestuous siblings. This was all first posited by John Rhys in 1898[17]. Rhys is one of the greatest scholars ever to work on Celtic literature, and was a genius, but he was also sometimes too mono-mythaic (obsessed with linking all myths into one great story). In my opinion, this instance was one of those times, and that the idea still has currency only because of the unprofessional desire to connect the authentic, historic pagan past of Britain with the heroic age fantasies of the early medieval period.

---

[16] The barely understood Old Irish knowledge of complicated surgical procedures is unfortunately unparalleled in the extant Welsh literature, but would be an important factor for any future Irish version of this book.
[17] *Celtic Britain*, pp.123-5

The Case of Gorsedd Arberth

Introduction

The word 'gorsedd' has a range of meanings in the Brittonic languages. The word in modern times is used in Wales, Cornwall and Brittany to describe the delegation of robed bards, druids and ovates seen at national gatherings (or at the Eisteddfodau in Wales) who were nominated for their abilities with the language and history of their respective regions. In standard Welsh the word refers to a throne or high seat. However in the earlier language the normal use of the word is to describe a flat-topped hill, and the word is probably cognate with the Old Irish word 'síd', (fairy mound).

There is not such a strong tradition of non-humans living inside these mounds in medieval Welsh literature as in Irish and Norse literature, perhaps because the Welsh word 'gorsedd' also covers natural humps and hillocks as well as burial barrows. However these mounds are still perceived as eerie places where things out of the ordinary will happen. This may be in part because of the shared archaeological heritage of Britain and Ireland. In Bronze Age Europe people, particularly those part of the so called "Beaker Culture" were often buried in "round barrows". These are small artificially made hills, raised over the top of human burials. Some of these, particularly in places where they are of high density like on the Salisbury Plain are still visible today, and many more would have been visible in early medieval times. It was also the custom of the "Anglo Saxon" culture in Britain early on in the sixth and seventh centuries to raise barrows over their own dead, so the function of the much earlier mounds would have been obvious to them. There is even a story in Old English of how one was created over the cremated remains of Beowulf at the end of his saga. That's not all either. In the Neolithic – the last "Stone Age" before the Bronze Age in Britain, "long barrows" were used. These were meant for the burial of large groups of people as opposed to the single use of the round barrow. They had entrances (albeit ones usually sealed by large slabs of stone) and many of these, as for example Knowth and Newgrange in Ireland and West-Kennet Long Barrow and Wayland's Smithy in Britain are still structurally sound enough to enter, although they have required some refurbishment over the years. It seems probable that legends about these barrows in Ireland and Wales were part of the oral tradition of the country. These barrows were not used in the medieval period, although cairns were still being built up to the very early medieval period. However the legends about them probably constitute a sort of folkloric memory, amplified by the Anglo-Saxon practice (before their conversion to Christianity).

ENTRANCE TO THE GREAT CAIRN OF NEW GRANGE, ON THE BOYNE, NEAR DROGHEDA

Newgrange Long Barrow entrance-way, shown before it was "restored".
This is approximately how it would have looked in medieval times.

Image originally from Charles Squire's *Celtic Myth and Legend*, 1905.

The last long barrow i named, Wayland's Smithy, although not as impressive as the other examples is interesting in that its very name preserves an Old English myth about the place. Wayland was a great smith in Norse mythology, and was also known in Old English ("Anglo-Saxon") mythology as well (he is mentioned in 'Beowulf' and a couple of shorter poems). Local folklore of the place suggests anyone whose horse has lost a shoe can leave a coin and their horse at the mound to have it re-shoed by the next day. Whether this myth was around in medieval times or represents a more modern invention is impossible to know, but the existence of the name suggests that people believed Wayland lived in the place, or at least returned there to work. This sort of tentative linking of barrows with heroes and legendary characters is typical of the medieval British imagination.

The most discussed 'gorsedd' in medieval Welsh literature is probably the Gorsedd Arberth, which is the subject of our case study. Arberth, as it is called in Middle Welsh is clearly a name for the still-existing town called "Narberth" in Pembrookshire, and the gorsedd could be any of the various knolls around the town. Although Gorsedd Arberth is alone in Medieval Welsh legend as having this folklore, it seems probable to me that originally other gorsedd were also known as supernatural or liminal places. However Gorsedd Arberth is clearly quite an important example and is mentioned four times in the first and third branches of the 'Mabinogi' ('Pwyll' and 'Manawydan'). It sets the scene for all of the most important interactions with a "magician" called Llwyd Cil Coed. This character is known from Old Irish literature, and Pryderi's antagonistic relationship him perhaps mirrors the relationship of his father, Pwyll to Arawn of Annwfn. The parallel is made even clearer when we learn that this magician is just one of a whole race of people with strange abilities. Others connected to his race include Rhiannon, whom many scholars have suggested reflects a euhemerised pagan deity (her case is approximately equal in strength to that of Lludd which I described in "the Case of the Coranieid"). Ultimately I have decided not to consider this long plot line as a separate case in its own right. Compared to the people from Annwfn, stories featuring Llwyd Cil Coed's family have no strange titles, no early reference in old poetry, and, looking at the broad picture, the story looks more like a modern soup opera than a legend. I believe that this storyline was based upon the strange tales of Annwfn, but has little likelihood of containing lost intelligence about historic aliens. There are however, a few times when the story seems to draw on older topoi, not preserved elsewhere. In my opinion, one of these is the magician's association with a gorsedd, which I would suggest was also originally found in the "Case of Arawn of Annwfn". I have also translated another part of the story connected to Llwyd Cil Coed in "Cases of Powerful Artefacts".

There are four main references to the Gorsedd Arberth that I am aware of in Medieval Welsh literature, one in the 'The First Branch of the Mabinogi' ('Pwyll') and three in the third ('Manawydan'). The 'Four Branches of the Mabinogi' are of course Medieval Welsh staples and their language is datable to the eleventh and twelfth centuries. The original text can be found edited in *Pedeir Keinc y Mabinogi* by Ifor Williams and is translated well in any one of the many books called *The Mabinogion*.

The Texts

1.

One day, he [Pwyll] was in Arberth, his chief-court, and a feast had been readied for him, and great retinues of men together with. And after the main course, Pwyll arose to journey forth, and he went to the top of the gorsedd that was above [and] to one side of the court, that was called Gorsedd Arberth.

'Lord,' said one of the court, 'it is a property of this gorsedd, that whichever nobleman may sit on it, he shall not go from it without one of two things, either his striking or wounding, or he himself may see a wonder.'

'I have no fear of getting struck or wounded, among this retinue. [As for] a wonder however, I would like it if I saw one! – I shall go,' he said 'to sit on the gorsedd.'

He sat on the gorsedd, and while they were sitting [there], they saw a woman on a large, pale, high horse, with golden, shining clothes of brocaded silk around her. [She was] coming along the highway that wandered past the side of the gorsedd.

Our first text is the only one from 'Pwyll' and also perhaps the most useful of the extracts. It comes directly after the end of the extract we looked at in 'Arawn of Annwfn'. One of the most interesting lines is the first one in the second paragraph which explains specifically that it is a 'kynnedyf' (natural law, custom, property) of *this* gorsedd that anyone sitting on it may see a marvel or be wounded. This implies that the same cannot be said for every gorsedd, although it is possible that many gorseddau had their own properties.

The exact wonder that he sees is interesting as well. The well-dressed woman is Rhiannon, who I mentioned in the introduction as one of the people connected with Llwyd Cil Coed. This leads us to the suggestion that perhaps being on top of the gorsedd allows a person to see the people of the gorsedd on their day to day business who are normally invisible. This would certainly resonate with Gaelic legends and folklore, where often the people of the síd are only viewable by those who have been into their mounds, or perhaps on Hallowe'en (old Samhain).

2.

And they started to feast in Arberth, since it was the chief court, and from it every honour began. And after the first course of that night while the servants were eating they went out, and all four of them made for Gorsedd Arberth and their retinue together with them. And while they were sitting thus, behold a tumult [came] and because of the greatness of the tumult, behold, a bank of mist came until no one of them could see his companions. And after the mist, behold, everything brightened. And when they looked the direction they had seen herds and the droves, and the dwelling places before that, [now] no-one saw anything at all, neither houses, nor animals, nor pigs, nor fires, nor people, nor dwellings, except the empty houses of the desolate, uninhabited court. [They were] without people, without animals within them, having lost their own companions without knowing anything of them save [only] the four of them...

Our second text comes from near the beginning of 'Manawydan'. During 'Pwyll', Pwyll marries Rhiannon, the character he sees in the first text, and they have a son, Pryderi, who accompanies Manawydan on this adventure. Also present are Rhiannon (who probably should have known better than to visit this mound) and Kicua, Pryderi's wife. The trouble is that before Rhiannon married Pwyll, she was promised to another (Gwrawl). He was tricked out of having her by Pwyll, and beaten by Pwyll's men, and this has made Llwyd Cil Coed want vengeance for the insult to his friend. Part of his vengeance is enchanting the land of Dyfed in the way described in this passage. I have considered this passage in more detail in "Cases of Strange Sounds".

3.

One morning, Pryderi and Manawydan arose to hunt; and ready their hounds, and go out from [Arberth] court. This is what a few of the hounds did, walking ahead of them, and going to a little thicket [that] was near at hand. And as they went to the thicket, they exit with speed, with their great bristles standing on end from terror, and return to the men. 'Let us approach,' said Pryderi, '[to the] side of the thicket, to see what is inside.' They approached towards the thicket. When they approached, behold: a shining wild boar coming from the thicket; here is what the hounds did, with the encouragement of the men, charging to it. This is what it did: leaving the thicket, and retreating a little before the men. And before the men were near to it, [it was] holding the hounds at bay without retreating from them, and when the men closed, [it was] retreating again and breaking away.

And they went after the boar, until they saw a great fortress over-head, and [it was] newly built, in a place they had not ever seen a stone or [any] construction; and the boar headed swiftly to the fortress, and the dogs after it. And after the boar went with the dogs into the fortress, they were surprised to see the fortress in a place [that] they had not ever seen construction before that, and from the top of the gorsedd they looked, and awaited the dogs.

In the third passage Manawydan and Pryderi are hunting in the wilderness left of Dyfed after the enchantment explained in the second passage. The white boar they decide to follow is clearly an otherworldly creature (there is a common motif in Welsh legends that people can follow a white boar or stag into the Otherworld). The gorsedd is not especially obvious in this story, but it is interesting in that Manawydan and Pryderi do not seem to have seen the fortress before (it later vanishes) nor do they seem to see it at all until they are very close to the gorsedd. Perhaps it is another marvel, which they see only because they are on the gorsedd. What scholars would call "in a liminal zone".

Image by WestWalesP, freely licensed for use under GFDL v1.2. See:
http://commons.wikimedia.org/wiki/Commons:GNU_Free_Documentation_License_1.2
Picture shows Narberth Castle, possibly the castle refered to in the preceding extract. However, it was only built in the thirteenth century, so either the story is a late interpolation or the text originally refered to a different castle.

4.

'What is that, Lord?' Said Kicva.

'A thief,' he said, 'which i caught stealing from me.'

'What kind of thief, Lord, could you keep in your glove?' said she.

'This is it:' he said, and he explained about the contamination and the destruction of his crofts, and about

[how] the mice had come to him to the last croft in his presence.

'And one of them was fat, and I caught it, and it is that in the glove, and I shall hang it tomorrow. And by my oath to God, if I caught all of them, I would hang them!'

'Lord ,' said she, 'that is natural. And yet it is unseemly to see a man as good [and] as noble as you hanging that kind of vermin. And if you would do right, you would not concern yourself with the vermin, except to let it escape.'

'Woe to me,' he said 'if I did not hang as many as I caught, if I caught them all!'

'Well Lord,' said she, 'there is no need for me to be supporting that vermin, except to prevent your being dishonoured. You do your own will, Lord.'

'If I myself knew of any reason in the world for you to support it, I would take your counsel about it, but since I don't know [of any], Lady, My thought is to destroy it.'

'You do that happily,' said she.

And then he went to Gorsedd Arberth, and the mouse with him, and raised two forks in the highest place on the gorsedd. And while he was thus, behold, he saw a scholar coming to him, and old, worn out, pauper clothes. And 'twas seven years before that that he had seen either man or animal except the four-people that were with him, until he [had] lost two.

Extract four is our final part of the story, but it needs so much explanation that I have quoted more than just the part about the gorsedd at the end. Our text here comes directly after the extract I have given in "Cases of Strange Sounds". The mouse Manawydan has caught is one of Llwyd Cil Coed's people transformed into a mouse in order to steal his wheat. According to native Welsh law, Manawydan has the right to hang any thief he caught in the act, especially since they came at night. However, this law does not apply to animals, and it seems quite clear that Manawydan knows that the mouse is a transformed human, although he does not explain this to Kicua. Similarly, I think we must take his decision to hang the mouse on Gorsedd Arberth to be a very cynical move. As I have explained, the gorsedd seems to act as a liminal place where noblemen can see into the Otherworld. By setting up the gallows there, Manawydan is ensuring that Llwyd knows about it. In fact, he is entirely vindicated in his assumptions. The mouse turns out to be Llwyd's own pregnant wife, carrying his unborn son, and after a number of people (probably Llwyd in disguise) go past and try to buy the mouse from Manawydan for an increasing price, Llwyd finally reveals himself and offers to undo all of his magic and give up on his revenge, which brings the 'Third Branch of the Mabinogi' to a happy ending.

Interpretation

Before we move on much further with the Interpretation I should point out once again the soap-opera-like nature of this entire storyline in general and the final scene in particular. What starts out as a chance meeting turns into a marriage, which becomes a grave insult and insult turns into revenge, which all culminates in Manawydan standing on a gorsedd preparing to hang a mouse. The farcical nature of this last scene would surely not be lost on a medieval audience, and was probably meant to be funny. Needless to say I do not believe there is very much of historical significance here. However, the motif of the gorsedd does seem to be used very well by the writer.

Overall Gorsedd Arberth appears to function as a liminal zone. This means that it is a place in which this world and the Otherworld can meet. People can see through and sometimes travel through to the other side. That is the standard explanation for the significance of any gorsedd, or barrow or síd but especially Gorsedd Arberth. But is this all there is to this motif? If so there is no particular need to bring in aliens at all. We have a group of monuments, tentatively associated with people from times long past, upon which strange things are said to happen. The monuments have a reputation as places from which you can see strange things, but upon which you may get into trouble, rather like a graveyard, castle or "haunted house" at night.

On the other hand, if aliens were visiting the Earth these old monuments might be good places to stay. They would be visible from the air and they are often purposefully aligned to a cardinal direction or to a solar event which would help with navigation. This is especially the case for long-barrows which is why Newgrange needs its own lottery to decide who will be allowed to view the sunrise of the winter solstice from within. Barrows also tend to be in sparsely populated areas, although this is obviously not true of Arberth Gorsedd which is described as directly above a busy Welsh court complex. Finally barrows might represent the very last obvious signs of Neolithic civilisation in Britain. This is significant for three reasons. If aliens visited only sporadically, these might be the only familiar places left. If aliens established bases underground, which seems to be suggested by, for example, "The Case of 'Preiddeu Annwfn'" and traditional Irish stories of síd with people living in them, it is possible that locations under burial mounds, would have been quite good choices, especially if they had secret ways to enter their bases through the open barrows.

Ultimately though, this sort of speculation is quite far removed from our evidence, and there is most likely nothing to these ideas. Sadly therefore we have to consider the "Case of Gorsedd Arberth" as our least successful case-file, and one which most likely contains no secret knowledge or information about ancient aliens. I do think it needed to be considered especially given the references to 'Síd' in "The Case of 'Preiddeu Annwfn'" and the importance of one of the Gorsedd Arberth texts in the "Cases of Strange Sounds". Altogether it is more useful to have combed it for references to aliens and then discounted it than not to have considered it at all. Thankfully our next case is not nearly so barren.

Cases of UFOs in 'The Anglo-Saxon Chronicle'

Introduction

Contrary to popular belief, the science of astronomy was well understood in ancient times. In medieval Britain and Ireland the first six planets of our solar system were known, together with the sun, Milky Way and a few other stars[18]. Mercury, Venus, Earth, Mars, Jupiter and Saturn were known, and it was also known (by the most learned) that they are in a heliocentric system in that order. 'Ieuan's Boast' a poem from the fifteenth century even talks about the use of the astrolabe and quadrant to study the positions of *seven* planets (perhaps including the moon and the sun but not the Earth). Together with this, and knowledge of comets and eclipses, medieval people were also familiar with the astrology of the zodiac which still endures to this day. This means that medieval accounts of celestial bodies can incorporate both reasonably educated and scientific testimonies of observed phenomena, and superstitious declarations interpreting the future at the same time. In addition, as well as the personal astrology of the zodiac which allowed people to foretell the future of individuals, certain signs foretold the future for everyone. At any given time, a particular planet in a particular phase in the sky would have the main influence over the world, which meant that certain dates were more predisposed towards war or peace for example. Finally, in medieval Christianity, changes in the heavens which were visible with the naked eye (especially comets) were usually thought to foretell ruin, war and famine. The end of the world was also still expected (this is the doctrine of "imminent parousia") and certain astrological signs were expected to precede it.

Unfortunately for our circumstances, this means that even in supposedly "historical" literature, many of the celestial signs mentioned did not actually occur when they were supposed to, and are instead inserted for dramatic effect[19]. However this need not concern us much

---

[18] See: Mark Williams, *Fiery Shapes* for information about medieval Celtic knowledge of astronomy (especially p.3; p.10; p.84-5) and a general study of astrological knowledge in medieval Irish and Welsh literature.

for two reasons. First of all, when astronomical events are described for dramatic effect this is often very obvious, as the event will immediately precede or succeed the description of a war of death of a great man. I have included an example of this in the extract below. Secondly, just like in the fiction we have studied throughout this book, even if any given astronomical event is fictional, it may still draw on motifs and details of real events. This is especially probable when the event in question is described in exact detail. In cases like this, the account of the fictional event is very likely to have been inspired by the description of a previous real event.

Obviously this chapter is a little different to the majority of the rest of the book. The text I am translating was written in a late stage of Old English (some of it potentially an early stage of Middle English). In addition, since it is discussing physical phenomena I have inserted a few photos for comparison. I hope that these will allow readers to decide for themselves whether the astronomical events described are natural or whether they could represent anything more.

The first version of the 'Anglo-Saxon Chronicle' was probably written in 892 A.D. That version seems to be lost, but was probably the first to incorporate events from 60 B.C. up until 892 A.D., a text which is a feature found in our earliest extant versions. Despite this early start however, the majority of the information up to the fifth century is made up of Biblical and general Roman history. The 'Chronicle' only acquires its British focus after 449, when the "Saxons Angles and Jutes" arrive (perhaps naturally). From 892 until the eleventh century many other versions begin. They copy the oldest information from other chronicles, and then continue writing independently and contemporaneously with the events they describe. After the eleventh century the chronicles are abandoned one by one.

The 'Anglo-Saxon Chronicle' has many editions, but our main extracts come from 'Recension E' or the 'Laud Chronicle' which is the name given to the version of the text found in <u>Bodleian Laud Misc. 636</u> at Oxford. This version preserves the very last years of the chronicle, from which come most of our references. This version was created after a fire destroyed the Peterborough monastery, and possibly the original

---

[19] See *Fiery Shapes*, pp.xiii-xiv

version of the chronicle there in 1116. Perhaps to replace the version lost, the scribes created a new version which is written in hybrid of the northern and eastern dialects. The last entries also begin to resemble Middle English more and more making it obvious that the entries with an earlier date were not written at the same time. The text can be found edited online individually here and translated separately in *The Peterborough Chronicle,* but any book called *The Anglo Saxon Chronicle* will usually incorporate the entries of this chronicle, together with all the other chronicles.

The Texts

793

This year there were wild forebodings coming over the land of the Northumbrians, and these terrified the folk horribly. These were great [amounts of] sheet lightning and fiery dragons flying among the clouds. The tokens [were] immediately followed [by] much hunger and a little after these [things] in the same year, on the sixth of the ides of January, horribly heathen men wreaked destruction [on] God's church on Lindisfarne through plunder and slaughter.

Our extract from 793 A.D. is the only one of our entries which is duplicated in other versions of the 'Chronicle'. It is found in the 'Worcester Chronicle', which was written in the eleventh century but the entry itself may be older, although since it is not present in our oldest extant chronicles it was certainly not written by contemporaries of the time. It also possibly inspired a similar scene in 'Historia Regum Britanniae' which we shall compare later.

I should explain the confusing medieval calendar system used here before going much further. The ides of a month is a date in the middle of it, usually the 13th but the 15th in the case of March, May, July and October. The calends of a month is the first day of it. When numbers are given, they are counted backwards from the day itself. Therefore, when the Old English Writers describe 'the sixth of the ides', they are referring to five days before it (since the day itself is the 'first of the ides'). Therefore the 'sixth of the ides of January' is the 8th of January. This is quite strange since we are told all the events happened 'ilcan geares' (in the same year). It seems quite peculiar that this storm and the famine could have taken place in just a week, so it is possible that the author intended to write the 'sixth of the calends of January' (or the 26th of December).

This particular entry has inspired lots of discussion. The word 'forbecna' (forebodings) quite succinctly demonstrates how medieval people in Britain saw strange astrological phenomena: They are signs or warnings of woe to come. Professor Swanton, one of the greatest living scholars of Old English has suggested that these dragons should be seen as long tailed comets[20], and the lightning could be cloud-to-cloud lightning, which never touches the ground and often appears to be more violent than cloud-to-ground lightning. See pictures below for examples:

Image by Fir0002/Flagstaffotos, freely licensed for use under GFDL v1.2. See:
http://commons.wikimedia.org/wiki/Commons.GNU_Free_Documentation_License_1.2

---

[20] *The Anglo Saxon Chronicle,* p.54.

1882 Nov 7ᵈ

Picture of the Great Comet of 1882 photographed by the South African Astronomical Observatory. Note the long streaking tail. Occasionally the main body of the comet can be seen in more detail, so it is clear which direction the comet is going.

As Professor Swanton rightly points out, this lightning can suddenly light up clouds so that they appear lit up in strange relief like the cloud in the centre of the first picture above, and therefore our annal entry could easily reflect a memory of this kind of storm. I am dubious of his idea that the dragon could be a just a long-tailed comet however. There are nine comets recorded in the 'Anglo Saxon Chronicle' between 678 and 1097 (although only five of these appear in our E version). Now these comets are described in good detail, occasionally complete with their 'fæxedon' (long hair/tail). This suggests at least a basic competence in star gazing, and therefore, it seems likely that the scribe would have recorded his dragons as a comet if it was one. That the sighting was recorded as a dragon strongly suggests that the scribe witnessed some other, as yet unexplained phenomenon.

On the other hand, it also seems probable that this narrative was written for the purpose of creating a dramatic backdrop to the Viking attack on Lindisfarne, which was one of the most important abbeys in Britain at the time. Therefore it is quite possible that the dragons are in fact meant to be taken as dragons and nothing more.

1100

Thereafter in the month of June, a star appeared [due] north-east, and it its beam stood in front of it in the south-west. Thus it was seen many nights and as the night grew later it rose higher. It was seen going back towards the north-west.

The rest of our annals are from the twelfth century and attested only in the E version of the 'Chronicle'. Although as I have said, the medieval inhabitants of Britain had a practical astronomical knowledge, their common vocabulary did not distinguish much between various astronomical sightings. The word 'steorra' (star) is ambiguous, and can refer to any light in the sky. This is still the custom in Modern English when we use our word, 'star', to refer to any of the pinpricks of light in the sky regardless of whether they are stars, other systems or galaxies. Even comets were often called comet-stars just like we might call them "shooting-stars".

In the annal entry from 1100 we have a classic UFO moment with a star moving in a way it should not. Anyone driving at night knows that this is a fairly common occurrence, although a UFO being seen for many consecutive nights is more unusual. Interestingly it is not identified as a comet, which is strange given its tail. Meteorites of course fall in showers and would not be visible for nearly so long.

1106

In the first week of Lent on the Friday, the fourteenth of the calends of March, in the evening an unusual star appeared, and [for a] while thereafter, each evening it was seen shining. The star appeared in the south-west [and] it was low magnitude and dark, but the ray of light that stood

from it was very bright and like an intense magnitude
beam shining north-east. One evening the beam was seen
as if it were thrusting forward against the star, flashing.
Some said that they saw more strange star[s] at this time
but we do not write unreservedly of it because we
ourselves did not see it. On the night [before] the morning
of 'Cena Domini', that is the Thursday before Easter, two
moons were seen in the heavens before the day, one due-
east, the other due-west, both full, this same was the
fourteenth day of the moon [i.e. the lunar month].

In the entry from 1106 we find another peculiar "star" seen on the
'fourteenth of the calends of March' (the 18th of February). Again this
one has a tail suggesting it may be a comet, but it is not listed as such,
suggesting that perhaps the author believed it must be something else.
The central part of the extract is quite hard to understand. A comet's
tail could not flash and quite how any tail could appear to be thrusting
off against the body of the "star" is hard to imagine. The refusal to
record the other 'uncuðra steorra' (unknown/"uncouth" stars) is also
interesting. It suggests that the author may have seen the two moons
and the first unusual star himself, and indeed that these stars may have
been even more peculiar. Finally, the record of two moons in the sky is
fascinating. Unless the viewer was looking out over a large body of
water I cannot explain it.

1117

This year moreover, in the night of the calends of
December there were tremendous tempests with thunder
and lightning and rain and hail. And on the night of the
third of the ides of December the moon was long [into the]

night as if it were all bloody and afterwards obscured.

Moreover on the night of the seventeenth of the calends of

January was the heaven seen very red as if it were burning.

I believe that all of the events described in the annal of 1117 are present to once again provide a dramatic backdrop to the events of the year (the oppression of Normandy). This is suggested by the bringing together of the astronomical observations with notes about tempests and later an earthquake and many deaths. In addition the phenomena described are all observable and explainable. The moon appears red quite often due to Rayleigh Scattering, especially when it is low on the horizon. When light enters through our atmosphere, many of the photons which make up its distinct colour become scattered. This is more likely to happen (and therefore happens more strongly) to higher-frequency blue (and sometimes violet) photons than lower-frequency yellow and red photons. This means that bodies outside our atmosphere are more disposed to appear red or orange than blue or violet. This is particularly the case when they are low on the horizon (from our perspective), as that means their light has to go further through our atmosphere to reach us. An example is the way a setting sun (on the horizon) will often seem red, even though it is normally yellow. See the diagram below.

Diagram of Rayleigh Scattering

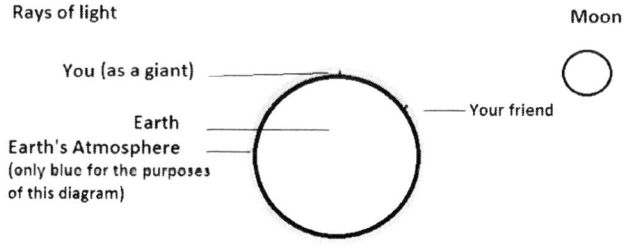

The moon will appear red to you because it has to go through so much atmosphere to reach you. It will appear normally to your friend because the photons not have to pass through so much atmosphere to reach them.

Likewise the sky can also appear red simply because of the northern lights. A significant appearance of the northern lights in England is quite rare, but once every eleven years, at the height of the Sun's cycle there is a good chance it can be seen across England, especially in Northumbria where this version of the chronicle was written. An entirely red version would be still rarer. The aurora borealis normally appears green, or mostly green, but purely red versions of the lights can be seen, as the photo below (taken at Swifts Creek, Australia).

Image by Fir0002/Flagstaffotos, freely licensed for use under GFDL v1.2. See:
http://commons.wikimedia.org/wiki/Commons:GNU_Free_Documentation_License_1.2

1122

Thereafter there were many shipmen at sea and on water and they said that they saw a large and broad fire by the earth wax its length up to the cloud, and the cloud undid itself into four parts, and fought there against it as if it would quench it. And the fire waxed regardless up to the heavens. They saw that fire at daybreak and it lasted as long as it was light overhead. That was the seventh day of the ides of December.

The annal entry from 1122 is one of the more perplexing in the entirety of the chronicles. The core of the difficulty is probably with the word 'wolcen'. This word has a cognate in the more modern English word 'welkin', however I have never seen this word outside of a dictionary and believe it to be archaic. According to the Oxford English Dictionary

Timeline, the word only has three senses attested before 1400, the firmament/heavens, the sky or a cloud. I should note that the latest reference given this word was in John Morris' poems in 1860, which suggests it has indeed become extinct. Having said that, the sense of 'cloud' in my opinion is the best translation for this context, since the 'wolcen' splits itself into pieces in our extract and the sky/firmament could not do that. I cannot think of any natural phenomenon resembling this description, but I have some speculations about it in the Interpretation section.

1131

This year after Christmas on a Monday-night at the first sleep, the heaven of the northern half was all as if it were a burning fire, so that all that saw it were as frightened as they never were before that. That was the third ide of January. The same year was a mighty cattle-plague as there never was before in man's memory across all England. That was on bovine and on swine, so that on the farm that there were ten plough[team]s or twelve going, there was left not one, and the man that had two hundred or three hundred swine had left to him not one. Thereafter the hen fowl perished, then the [supply of] meat shortened and the cheese and the butter.

Our last extract is from 1131. I believe this extract is entirely comparable with the annal of 1117, and is once again using descriptions of disasters to set up a sense of drama for the narrative. The burning sky could easily be another sighting, or a memory of a red aurora borealis[21].

---

[21] It is worth noting that all this happened 'at the first sleep', or quite early in the evening (somewhere between 6 and 11 o'clock P.M) an optimum time for northern lights sightings. In the medieval period many people slept twice

However, there is at least one other possibility. The idea of a plague together with natural disasters to me mirrors the symptoms we saw in "The Case of 'Marwnad Ithel ap Robert'". In that chapter I raised the possibility that all of the symptoms were caused by the arrival of the 'Eingl' from space. This annal, if written roughly contemporaneously with the events in purports to describe was written about 250 years before 'Marwnad Ithel ap Robert', but if the Eingl could have been responsible for the events there, they could equally have been responsible for the events in this text.

during the night, getting up between these "sleeps" for a meal, or to converse and take leisure. For more on the topic of divided sleep see *At Day's Close: Nights in Times Past* by A. Roger Ekirch.

Interpretation

Of the six annal extracts I have translated, I believe that one of them, our text from the year 1117 can be immediately dismissed based on my original commentary and attendant pictures. It discusses phenomena (red sky, a red moon, a storm) which are easily understandable (unusual red aurora borealis, Rayleigh Scattering, a storm). All these phenomena were most likely used for dramatic effect, and there is no need for them even to have occurred in tandem. Although the text is interesting in itself, it almost certainly has no significance for our purposes.

I suggest that the entry from 1131, which mentions a red sky and later a plague, also just contains descriptions of natural phenomena. It does bear a certain resemblance to the events described in Marwnad Ithel ap Robert, but the similarities are not striking enough to speculate about.

The entry from 1100 is more difficult. It forms quite a good UFO case report, but is tantalisingly brief in its details, and I know of no other source which mentions it. Unfortunately there is just not enough evidence to speculate on, but it does at least form an interesting comparison case for those who argue that our UFO reports are culturally specific.

The entry from 793 I believe to also have been written to give a dramatic context to the Viking attack on Lindisfarne Abbey island. However the motifs used, which were probably not original to this report are very interesting. The strange lightning referred to could well refer to sheet lightning, but for a reference to the dragon we may prefer to turn to Geoffrey of Monmouth's Latin 'Historia Regum Britanniae' from 1136 (i.e. probably written much later). There dragons represent dynasties, so that fighting dragons are interpreted as the defenders of the native Britons and of the Saxons, and when Aurelius Ambrosius dies another dragon is seen:

'Historia Regum Britanniae' Book VIII, Chapter 15.

Whilst these [things] occurred at Winchester, a star of great magnitude and clarity appeared, one ray extended, [and] truly, there was a globe of fire in the shape of a dragon stretched out, and out from this one's mouth emitted two rays, one of which [was] itself of such length that it seemed to extend beyond the climes of Gaul and another truly bent towards the Irish sea ending in seven lesser rays. Truly, by this appearance of this star, all are impelled to fear and wonder.

This dragon does not just represent the death of Aurelius Ambrosius, it also symbolises the start of a new dynasty, starting with Uther, who took the name Pendragon, "dragon-head", after this event. But obviously, if historical annals can be suspect of inserting wondrous stars just for dramatic effect, a dragon-star's appearance in this renowned fairytale "history" is far more suspect. Indeed I certainly do not believe that the appearance of this star actually happened upon the death of any great hero. However the repeated use of the motif suggests that it could represent a real remembered event, merely being used for the sake of the story. The rays of light in the 'Historia Regum Britanniae' account are also very interesting. The 'radium/i' (rays) seem not only reminiscent of a couple of the other annal entries but also suggest ray/laser weaponry which is only now beginning to be discovered by humanity. Boeing YAL-1 is a US Air Force which has successfully used lasers in test scenarios to stop missiles in mid-flight, either intercepting or destroying them. Unfortunately the lasers have quite a short range, meaning that the plane only has limited usage and so testing of the technology has ceased. Non-lethal "dazzlers" however have been far more accepted, and were issued to American troops in Iraq War of 2003. These are supposed to cause temporary blindness and confusion, although they have not been very successful at long range. On the other hand, these rays of light could just as easily represent very strong flashlight like Batman's famous Gotham City bat signal. With a bit of imagination, these rays could even describe the lightning weapons which may be remembered by the various magical weapons in "Cases of Powerful Artefacts".

To sum up, this motif of a star resembling a dragon seems to represent a recycled motif which may have had a real original basis. If so, the original event may reflect an alien spacecraft, although there is nowhere near enough evidence to make this any more than a speculation.

Having discussed the rays of light connected to the dragon-star, it is very interesting to find a very similar 'beam' of light connected to first strange star seen in 1106. There the ray is clearly being compared to a comet's tail, but to the viewer it seems wrong for a comet's tail – it is brighter than the comet itself, and it even seems to propel the craft at one point. This sounds amusingly like the twentieth century science fiction view of a "rocket ship", complete with yellow flames licking out the back to propel the craft onwards. Such a picture is still accurate for all of our space-faring vessels as they leave the atmosphere, but in space ships do not need to constantly accelerate. This has led most NASA spacecraft to separate from their initial launch vehicles (main rockets) as soon as they have left Earth's atmosphere. It is conceivable that a craft might retain its rockets for reuse, but it seems most likely that constant use of any rocket brighter than a comet's tail would entirely exhaust any possible fuel supplies.

The second UFO described in the 1106 annal is merely a second moon. I can easily imagine this being caused by an optical illusion, but if it was not, any such object would have to be huge. For example, the International Space Station is in low earth orbit. Any comet coming this close would almost certainly crash into Earth. However the International Space Station appears only as a very bright star, nowhere near as big as the moon. Any comet big enough to appear like a second moon (excluding the tail), unless it was very close indeed, would cause massive destruction and we would very certainly be aware of it if one like this had dropped in the last 2,000 years. What are the other possibilities then? There could have been an absolutely massive comet passing by, but no tail was reported, and the writer did not record this as a comet. Provided the object was not an optical illusion, did not have a tail, and lingered in the sky (i.e. was not an animal or insect), the only other explanation I can think of would be a spacecraft. Especially if the object was inside the atmosphere it need not be too big (consider the size of an airplane flying overhead), and if it had an intelligent controller there would be no need for it to crash.

Finally our extract from 1122 is the most probable annal to depict an alien presence. There is a great fire, which burns before waxing up into the sky (perhaps in a beam) and attacking the 'wolken' (cloud). This cloud then splits into four and attempts to 'acwencen' (quench/extinguish) the fire, which continues to wax up into the heavens. The fire continues all night although it is not clear this means that the fire continues its attack on the cloud, or just continues burning on the ground as it was previously. Other than this is it the detail of the account which really recommends itself to our circumstances. The way the cloud is describes ascribes it an agency and motivation which seems almost human, and the same is true, to a lesser extent, of the fire which leaps up. Could these phenomena be medieval aliens? If the answer is yes, the events certainly lend themselves to interpretation. The fire could have been a ground-to-air defence weapon, firing, and apparently overcoming, a disguised ship in the atmosphere. Such attacks are attested in our own stories of UFOs[22]. The cloud then proceeded to split into four parts, which is another common theme in our own stories. Finally the attempts by the clouds to quench the fire suggest perhaps that they fired at the base of the fire, although this part of the account lends itself to many different explanations.

Interestingly this is not the only account which assigns a 'wolcen' human-like intelligence. In the C version of the 'Anglo Saxon Chronicle', which is the second 'Abingdon Chronicle', another supposed cloud behaves very oddly:

> Chronicle C. 979
>
> The same year was seen a bloody cloud often in the
>
> likeness of fire that was appearing strongest at midnight.
>
> And it was outlined in misty beams, then dawn broke [and]
>
> then it slipped away.

---

[22] For example, the famous 'STS-48 video', filmed in September 1991 from the space shuttle Discovery. See:
(http://www.youtube.com/watch?v=eil_2WOv5VA) for a digitally enhanced version by the AlienXFiles.

This version of the annal was probably written in the middle of the eleventh century, but was almost certainly a copy of an earlier, now lost version. Some of the motifs in this account are once again familiar. The colour of the 'wolcen' suggests that perhaps we were too hasty in earlier discounting the red sky and moon depicted in the 1117 annal. Likewise the misty beams bring to mind the lasers that we discussed earlier.

It is also very interesting that these two references make up the only uses of the word 'wolcen' in any extant version of the 'Anglo Saxon Chronicle'. Could this suggest that the word was once used to describe any unidentified flying object? There is clearly great ambiguity in any term which can refer to the sky in general or a cloud in particular. Unfortunately, none of the handful of other references to 'wolcen' in Old English literature show comparable usage, so this idea must remain a theory. If I am right however, the existence of a term for the UFO phenomenon suggests it was culturally as visible to speakers of Old English as it was to speakers of Modern English.

This is probably a good place to finish our chapter on UFOs in Old English literature. Our findings are very interesting. To sum up, we have found that strange sky-borne phenomena form a frequently used topos in Old English literature, and were used to heighten tension in a narrative. This explains but, but not all of the sightings of such phenomena. The annals of 1122 and 1106 in particular give details of quite convincing sightings which are hard to explain with reference to currently scientifically understood phenomena alone. The annal of 793, although completely unconvincing in itself has a very interesting parallel in 'Historia Regum Britanniae' which suggests that the dragon featuring in it may represent the reuse of an older and more significant motif. Likewise the 1122 annal is paralleled in another anal from 979, which adds further significance to it, and the Old English word 'wolcen'. This interest in sky-borne phenomena, but a complete lack of interest in stories of terrestrial alien races mirrors the state of affairs in medieval Welsh, which we are looking at throughout the rest of the book. In medieval Welsh literature, as we have seen, the history and legends reflect a common belief that non-British and quite possibly non-human races of beings inhabited Britain in the past. However, with the exception of "The Case of 'Marwnat Ithel ap Robert'" these beings are never assigned any strange means of transport. When we do witness the arrival of such characters, they are usually transported on horses. These are often impressive horses, but never transport beyond human capability. On the other hand, there is some suggestion that originally this was not the case, and that the most extraordinary characters had unearthly technology with which they went from place to place. The following chapters will examine these suggestions.

Cases of Strange Sounds

Introduction

In medieval Welsh literature out-of-the-ordinary events in literature are very often preceded by a 'twrwf' (a strange, loud sound or 'tumult' as it is usually translated). This word comes to have fairly normal connotations in the late medieval literature tradition so that the examples in, for example, "The Case of 'Marwnad Ithel ap Robert'" are fairly innocuous. Even in the slightly chronologically earlier Middle Welsh "romances" (especially 'Geraint' and 'Peredur') the sound usually refers to the sound of the hooves of a heavy horse, or sometimes a thunder clap. However earlier on in the literature this was not the case, and the word usually referred either to the sound of armies and battle, or to a peculiar sound which precedes the arrival of strange person or event. It is this last usage for tumult that we are especially interested in.

With that in mind we will confine our attentions to just four texts. 'Pwyll' and 'Manawydan' are both 'Branches of the Mabinogi' and as I have discussed previously they can probably be dated to the eleventh or twelfth centuries. I have also given two extracts from the Middle Welsh romances, one from 'Peredur' (a Welsh version of the French 'le Conte du Graal') and one from 'Owain' (a Welsh version of the French 'Yvain'), although I should point out that the question of whether the French or Welsh versions of Arthurian texts are more "original" (often called the Mabinogionfrage) is still a very contended issue among medieval scholars. The date of the 'Owain' and 'Peredur' is still very uncertain but both texts are found in manuscripts from the fourteenth century, including the <u>White Book of Hergest</u> (Peredur is actually found in <u>Peniarth 7</u> from the thirteenth century). However, we have seen from the case of the 'Mabinogi' how much earlier texts can be than their containing manuscript and our extracts are specifically chosen for their anachronistic usage of the word 'twrwf', so the texts could be much older than this. The original texts of 'Pwyll' and 'Manawydan' can both be found edited in *Pedeir Keinc y Mabinogi* by Ifor Williams, the original text of 'Owain' can be found in *Owein* by R.L. Thomson and 'Peredur' can be found in *Historia Peredur vab Efrawc* by Glenys Goetinck. All of these texts can be found translated in most English versions of *The Mabinogion*.

The Texts

1. 'Pwyll'

This is what Teirnon did, rising and looking on the good size of the foal and while he was thus, he heard a great <u>tumult</u>, and after the sound, behold, a large claw [came] through the window to one side, and took hold of the foal by the mane. This is what Teirnon himself did, drawing a sword and [carefully] striking the arm at the point of the elbow, so that half of the arm and of the foal would be with him inside.

And, with that, he heard a <u>tumult</u>, and a scream at once. He opened the door and made a rush after the <u>tumult</u>. He did not see the [source of the] <u>tumult</u> because the night [was] so dark. But he kept a rush after it and pursued it. And a memory came to him that he had left the gate open so he returned. And to the gate, behold, a small boy in swaddling-clothes, having a mantle of brocaded silk wrapped around him. He took the boy to him and behold, the boy was strong for his age.

Our first extract is from the 'First Branch of the Mabinogi'. Teirnon is standing guard over a foaling mare because every year its foal gets stolen. The boy at the end of the extract is one who was kidnapped earlier on in the story, and therefore, although it is never explained, the claw may belong to a creature that abducts young creatures.

The use of the word 'twrwf' (tumult) in this context seems to come first when the creature arrives and then again when it goes to leave, suggesting that this is a noise made by the way that it travels. At the beginning of the second paragraph we hear that there was a tumult and a scream, insinuating that the tumult was not itself a scream. Oddly, the last use of the word suggests something that can be seen. This brings to mind the later use of the word to mean a melee, or the sound made by an army.

2. 'Manawydan'

And they started to feast in Arberth, since it was the chief court, and from it every honour began. And after the first course of that night while the servants were eating they went out, and all four of them made for Gorsedd Arberth and their retinue together with them. And while they were sitting thus, behold a tumult [came] and because of the greatness of the tumult, behold, a bank of mist came until no one of them could see his companions. And after the mist, behold, everything brightened. And when they looked the direction they had seen herds and the droves, and the dwelling places before that, [now] no-one saw anything at all, neither houses, nor animals, nor pigs, nor fires, nor people, nor dwellings, except the empty houses of the desolate, uninhabited court. [They were] without people, without animals within them, having lost their own companions without knowing anything of them save [only] the four of them...

... And when half the night had passed, behold, <u>the greatest</u> <u>tumult in the world</u>; this is what he did, looked. Behold there was a hoard of mice, and it was not possible for them to be counted or measured. And [although] he didn't know [it] then, the mice were falling upon the croft, and each one climbing up the stalk and bending with it and breaking the ear and biting through the ear and taking it, and leaving the stalk there. And he did not know that there was one stalk there on which there was not a mouse. And they made their way forth, each one with an ear. And then between anger and fury, he leapt among the mice. [But] he could not keep an eye on them any more than on the gnats or the birds of the air, except one which he saw was fat, which he thought was not able [to go faster] than a walk. He took off after that one, and he caught it and put it in his glove.

The first of our second extracts was one that we discussed earlier in 'The Case of Gorsedd Arberth'. It is again pivotal to our discussion, although for a completely different reason this time and so I have reproduced it. This time the tumult actually *causes* a bank of mist to descend. In this case it is possible that the 'twrwf' refers to a thunderclap, as it can do in the modern language. In this case we could be witnessing a storm at the top of a mountain. As anyone who does much walking or hiking will tell you, when you are quite high up storms can come in very fast. Once they have arrived, even if it is not raining at your height, visibility can be greatly reduced by the perspiration in the air. Sometimes people looking up at the peaks of mountains will describe them as "inside a cloud", and in effect this is true, and the same thing that reduces visibility for those inside the cloud themselves.

However I believe there is more to it than this. Normal storms do not magic away all the life in an area as this one seems to have done. Later on this is revealed to be the work of Llwyd Cil Coed, a character I referred to previously as probably invented in mimicry of Arawn Pen Annwfn. Therefore there is some justification for suggesting that the tumult may also have also announced the arrival of this character.

Our second extract comes with a horde of mice stealing Manawydan's grain. This theft is also later revealed to be the work of Llwyd Cil Coed, and the mice are revealed to be his family, magically transformed by him into mice. The tumult in this instance is again ambiguous. It probably refers to the movement of the mice, since mice, even individually can be noisy creatures. This would fit in with the other common use for the term 'twrwf' which describes the noise made by armies, especially ones going into battle. On the other hand, it is significant that the noise is the first thing which Manawydan hears of the creatures, which may suggest that once again it is their travelling which causes this noise.

3. 'Peredur'

And he heard the servants rising and clear the board of the chess pieces. And he heard a <u>great tumult</u>, and after the <u>tumult</u> he saw a large, black, one-eyed man coming inside. And the maidens rose to meet him and they removed his clothes from around him. And he himself went to sit, and after his senses came to him, and he had rested he looked at Peredur and asked who the knight [was].

Our third extract comes from 'Peredur'. In this text there are five uses of the term 'twrwf'. Two of them refer to the sound of horse hooves, one of them refers to the sound of a door opening (perhaps it should be assumed to have slammed shut?) and the last two are both in the extract I have given here. In this extract a rather unpleasant large black man returns home to find Peredur in his house (a disturbingly common incident for the simple Percival). It is his arrival that causes the great tumult. On the one hand this could easily be the sound of his horse, or indeed of his own footsteps in the manner of a fairy-tale giant. On the other hand the motif of this great, one eyed black man is a very old one in Welsh literature (seen also for example in 'Owain', and may be originally drawn from Irish portrayals of the Formorians) but it is not present in French literature, which suggests that this episode may be quite old. In this case perhaps the event should be taken at face value, and this man's arrival is simply preceded by a great sound, as seen in 'Pwyll'.

I should note, for the sake of those relatively new to medieval literature that the description of this man as a 'gwr du mawr' (big black man) probably means 'clad in black' rather than 'dark-skinned' – compare the better known case of the English 'Sir Gawain and the Green Knight'. Knights are very commonly described by either the colour of their armour or the colour of their hair. This text is set in an era before the trading of black slaves was common, and after European slaves had much value (with feudalism every lord kept his people in near-slavery anyway). If the man was supposed to be from a different continent this would probably have been said explicitly.

4. 'Owain'

Go up the hill until you reach the top. From there you will see a river-valley as if it were a great vale and in the centre of the valley you will see a great tree. And the tip is greener than the greenest pine-tree. And beneath that tree is a fountain. And in the middle of the fountain there is a marble slab. And on the slab there is a silver bowl from a silver chain, so they cannot be separated. And take the bowl and throw a bowlful of the water over the slab. And then you will hear a <u>great tumult</u> and you will think the sky and the earth is quaking with the <u>tumult</u>. And after the <u>tumult</u>, a very cold shower [so that] it will be difficult for you to stay alive. And the shower will be of hail and after the shower there shall be fine weather. And there won't be one leaf on the tree [which] is not carried away by the <u>tumult</u>, and with that, a shower of birds will come, and they will land on the tree. And you will never hear in your own country a song as good as they sing. And when you are most satisfied with the song of the birds, you will hear a panting and a groaning coming up to the side of the valley towards you. And with that, you will see a knight on a pure-black horse, wearing [a mantle of] pure-black brocaded silk around himself.

Our forth extract comes from 'Owain'. Here a character described identically to the black, one-eyed man in the previous extract is explaining to the listener what he needs to do to seek adventure. This extract is significant for its strange description of the fountain, and we shall return to consider that side of the story in more detail in "Cases of Powerful Artefacts". Again the uses of the word 'twrwf' in this account are ambiguous. Most translators since Lady Charlotte Guest have translated each use as 'a thunderclap', and indeed the tumult certainly does precede a very fierce storm in this story. However, the tumult also very definitely heralds the arrival of the black knight at the end of the story, and the use of the fountain is clearly meant to summon him, with the storm only the medieval version of a drum roll of suspense.

Interpretation

Although most of the examples I gave above seem confused about whether the 'twrwf' was the sound made by the arrival of a character, the sound of hooves or the sound of a thunder clap, I do not believe this in any way diminishes my argument. Indeed it seems perfectly clear to me that there was a motif early on that the arrival of supernatural characters was preceded by a 'twrwf'.

Extract number one, from 'Pwyll' contains this motif in its purest form. Teirnon is not chasing a thunderclap, and I do not believe that his 'tumult' is the sound of hooves either: First, we would probably be told if a horse was present, and Teirnon would not be able to keep up with a fleeing horse like he does the source of this sound. Finally only humans or beings that resemble humans, like ghosts or spirits, are able to ride horses in Welsh legends.

As I have said, the word 'twrwf' almost always refers to the sound of hooves in 'Geraint' and 'Peredur' and in later poetry. However, looking at the later uses, especially in 'Rhonabwy' and 'Peredur', people invariably seem to hear the sound of a 'twrwf' and then turn and see that it is a knight with a rider. This suggests to me that the tradition of 'twrwf' meaning "the sound of hooves" has its origins in the idea that supernatural characters make a sound when they arrive.

I believe our extract from 'Peredur' forms a proof of concept for this idea. The noise of the large black man arriving is ambiguous – does it refer to the sound of his hooves or is it just a simple otherworldly noise like we saw in 'Pwyll'? Either way it precedes the arrival of this supernatural character.

The second extract from 'Manawydan' I take to refer to a battle-tumult, which is another use of the word 'twrwf', attested quite early on. However, 'twrwf' can also refer to "a thunderclap", even in earliest texts. In these cases this sound is followed by a storm, just like a normal thunderclap often is. This is certainly the case in my first extract from 'Manawydan', and also in 'Owain'. This may have been the original meaning of 'twrwf', which later became confused into referring to just a loud sound (as in 'Pwyll'), or the sound of hooves (as elsewhere). It is also true that in our extract from 'Owain' especially, but also in our extract from 'Manawydan', the sound of the thunderclap heralds the arrival of supernatural creatures. The 'twrwf' in this instance is almost certainly 'a thunderclap' but also very often brings with it an alien entity. Is there a way to reconcile these two facts?

One elegant but intriguing explanation is that these alien species should be considered to have travelled on the storm, or perhaps to have caused a storm by their arrival. This has disturbing parallels with the natural disasters which we saw heralding the arrival of the 'Eingl' in "The Case of 'Marwnad Ithel ap Robert'". Either way, from the literature it is clear that the creatures are clearly travelling by their own volition and not by the whim of a natural storm. In 'Owain' for example, the storm would come as soon as the bowl of water was thrown on the marble slab. This happens more than once in the story, and it is clear that the bowl of water directly summons the storm, and ultimately the protector of the fountain. These supernatural characters are thus able to control the weather as well as travel on storms. I have found some hints that Indra and Varuna in Vedic Sanskrit literature may have been able to do this as well, which adds credence to the idea that perhaps real entities were observed travelling like this, inspiring the legends.

Of course, an alternative explanation would be that the arrival of the characters brings about a thunderstorm, but they themselves are travelling in physical space-craft. We all know that electric storms are caused when areas of high pressure meet areas of low pressure. Could a flying machine create an area of high pressure simply by moving very quickly? Alternatively, the explosive "sonic boom" created by breaking the speed of sound does sound something like a thunderclap, and would probably be described as such by those hearing it without understanding it. Human aeroplane technology from the second half of the twentieth century onwards has easily accomplished this speed and any alien species able to navigate to the Earth would almost certainly have the technology as well. Scientists are still investigating the possibility of breaking the sound barrier without a sonic boom by superheating the front of an aircraft, but this is such a hassle that it is possible that an alien species would not have cared enough to develop the technology. Perhaps the tumult originally just referred to a sonic boom without necessitating any storm at all, but as the motif was reused the thunderclap announcing the arrival of an entity suggested to the minds of some storytellers a storm of rain.

Thrust SSC (super-sonic car) the first manned land craft to break the speed barrier (in 1997) and still the holder of the World land-speed record.
Image by CMglee, licensed under the GNU v1.2. See:
http://commons.wikimedia.org/wiki/Commons:GNU_Free_Documentation_License_1.2

Cases of Powerful Artefacts

Introduction

This chapter translates multiple episodes which all have strange artefacts in them. It is my contention that although many of these artefacts are clearly plot devices or ideal versions of items already existing, some of them seem to describe technology which humans have discovered since then. This strange anachronism is especially peculiar in cases where the same or a very similar artefact is described in different sources, implying that it may have been generally known, despite the fact that it had not yet been invented by humanity. I realise that examining all of these artefacts together I am taking material out of context, but in my opinion this matters less when the only thing I am interested in is the strange artefacts present in any given text, rather than any subtlety of the plot. Because the texts come from very different manuscripts I shall write a slightly longer introduction to describe them all.

Our first text comes from 'Manawydan' which is 'The Third Branch of the Mabinogi'. As one of the branches of that text it shares the exact same provenance as Pryderi, which I explained in "The Case of Arawn of Annwfn". To briefly reiterate, there are two main manuscripts, The White Book of Rhydderch and The Red Book of Hergest, both of which are from the fourteenth century, but the language is believed to date from the eleventh or twelfth century. Part of 'The Third Branch' is also found in Peniarth 6 from the thirteenth century, which partially supports this theory. The standard edition is Ifor Williams' 'Pedeir Keinc y Mabinogi' and a good translation can be found in any version of *The Mabinogion*.

Our second and third texts is from 'Owain'. Like I commented in "Cases of Strange Sounds" this text is hard to date, but it must precede the manuscript tradition of the fourteenth century. The standard edition is *Owein* (a variant spelling) which is the Dublin Institute of Advanced Studies version by R.L. Thomson. It is translated in most English versions of The Mabinogion

Our fourth and eleventh texts come from 'Branwen' which is 'The Second Branch of the Mabinogi', and therefore usefully has exactly the same manuscript tradition, standard editions and translations as 'Manawydan'. However, should comment that Caswallon, the main character of our first extract is also described in many of the triads, and in 'Historia Regum Britanniae' and various other places, and may be partially based on Casivellaunus, the tribal leader who led the Britons against the Romans in 54 B.C. The rebellion by Caswallon described in our text is actually integral to the plot of Branwen and he continues to be the king of Britain in 'Manawydan', the first text above.

Our fifth and sixth texts both come from 'The Dream of Rhonabwy'. This text has always been among the least favourites of the Middle Welsh prose texts. It is almost unique among these in missing an easily obtainable modern standard edition for English speakers, but R. Williams *Breuddwyd Rhonabwy* for Welsh speakers is good, if quite hard to get hold of. It is translated in most versions of *The Mabinogion* along with the other Middle Welsh prose legends, but even in medieval times it seems to lack popularity, and it only present in the Red Book of Hergest, not the White Book of Rhydderch in the fourteenth century. From the historical context of the story (it is set in a united Powys in the twelfth century) the text can probably be dated to either between 1132-60 AD or (less likely) later, between 1263 and the date of the manuscript in 1382. The story seems to have had a written rather than oral original, but it is probable that the Red Book version was not the original story since some parts of the story appear to have become confused.

Our seventh extract comes from 'Lludd a Llefelys', which is the story we looked at earlier in "The Case of the Coranieid". As I said then, this text's manuscript tradition dates from the early thirteenth century (it's found in the Llanstephan 1 manuscript), and the text's genesis was probably sometime in the century leading up to that. Our focus this time is on the third oppression on the island where no food lasts in the king's court longer than a single day because someone is stealing it, and our extract concerns the method by which he is able to do so, without anyone seeing him.

Our eighth text comes from 'Culhwch ac Olwen'. Culhwch is found with the rest of the texts translated in the English *Mabinogion* in The Red

Book of Hergest and The White Book of Rhydderch, giving it a fourteenth century manuscript tradition. However the main body of the text as we have it is linguistically older than the text of the main 'Four Branches of the Mabinogi' and this probably gives the text a tenth or eleventh century date, although the text seems to have been influenced after this point by the material found in 'Historia Regum Britanniae', written around 1136. The tale contains some of the very oldest prose in the language, and has a lot of features apparently preserved from an Old Welsh (rather than Middle Welsh) version. The story is very peculiar and some plot exposition might be in order. The hero of our story, Culhwch, grows up and falls in love with Olwen, the daughter of Ysbaddaden Penkawr. This latter man is a terrible giant, so Culhwch goes to ask "The Emperor Arthur" to help Culhwch win Olwen. At this point approximately a sixth of the text is then passed listing the names of people that would have Arthur help Culhwch. He agrees to do so, locates the girl and then another sixth of the text is spent with Ysbaddaden listing a series of Herculean tasks which he wishes to see completed before he will consent to the marriage. Only a handful of these are completed in the text as we have it before the couple are wed and Ysbaddaden is killed. Our extract comes from the centre of the list of tasks, and concerns the gathering of some fabled artefacts which are required for the wedding ceremony and feast.

Our ninth text is a discrete work by itself and not part of any other story. It is translated and edited in various places, the easiest of which to obtain is 'Trioedd Ynys Prydein' by Rachel Bromwich. Her edition is becoming slightly out of date with the discovery of different versions of the text, but has been updated in newer editions and is still used because the volume collects so many other miscellaneous texts. Sadly for our circumstances this text is quite late. Its earliest form seems to be in Peniarth 51, which is a fifteenth century text. However, some of the "treasures" named in the text may be of far greater antiquity.

Our tenth text is from 'Preiddeu Annwfn'. As I said in the introduction to "The Case of 'Preiddeu Annwfn' this text is very difficult to date. It must have been written between 850 and 1250 (in the Old Welsh period). On the one hand the language seems very antique, but on the other, the references seem very late. Erring on the side of caution I would date this text to the twelfth century.

Our eleventh text comes from 'Branwen', see the introduction to text four above.

Finally, just before we start I would like to note my naming conventions. Each of the cases in the text extract has been given an <u>Underlined Title</u>. Some of these titles are quotes from the texts, and the last title 'The Thirteen Treasures of the Island of Britain' is supplied by the text. With the exception of this last title, and the underlined artefacts in the extract from Culhwch however, none of the titles are original to the medieval period.

The Texts

1. The Paralysing Hanging-Bowl in 'Manawydan'

When he came to the fortress, not a person, nor an animal, nor a boar, nor a hound, nor a house, nor a dwelling did he see in the fortress. He saw, in approximately the centre of the floor of the fortress, a fountain and work of marble-stone around it. And on the edge of the fountain, a basin (a golden one attached to four chains at that) above the slab of marble stone, and the chains going to the air, and he could not see an end of them. He himself was enraptured at how fine the gold [was], and how fine the work of the bowl [was], and came to [where] the bowl was and took hold of it. And as soon as he touched the bowl, both his hands stuck to the bowl, and his feet to the slab that he was standing on, and took his speech from him so that he was not able to say one word. And he stood thus.

Pryderi, the main character of this story was lured into this castle by a pure white wild boar, a sure sign that it is otherworldly. His hounds chased the creature into the castle, and didn't come out again, explaining why boars and hounds are mentioned in the first sentence of our text. The rest of the text is just as interesting. Hanging bowls are very remarkable artefacts in the archaeological record, and are generally only seen between the fourth and seventh centuries. Historically hanging bowls tend to be made of bronze, or occasionally silver, but other than this the description seems like it might reflect a picture, find, or memory from when the bowls were actually in use[23]. As

---

[23] See Laing & Laing, *Celtic Britain and Ireland: The Myth of the Dark Ages*, pp.213-4.

I have said, there is very little possibility that the text as we have it was this old, but it's possible that this single motif has been copied from much older times.

2. The Summoning Hanging-Bowl in 'Owain'

And beneath that tree is a fountain. And in the middle of the fountain there is a marble slab. And on the slab there is a silver bowl from a silver chain, so they cannot be separated. And take the bowl and throw a bowlful of the water over the slab. And then you will hear a great tumult and you will think the sky and the earth is quaking with the tumult. And after the tumult, a very cold shower [so that] it will be difficult for you to stay alive. And the shower will be of hail and after the shower there shall be fine weather. And there won't be one leaf on the tree [which] is not carried away by the tumult, and with that, a shower of birds will come, and they will land on the tree. And you will never hear in your own country a song as good as they sing. And when you are most satisfied with the song of the birds, you will hear a panting and a groaning coming up to the side of the valley towards you. And with that, you will see a knight on a pure-black horse, wearing [a mantle of] pure-black brocaded silk around himself.

Extract two from 'Owain', is one that we already considered briefly in the last chapter. Its relevance to us in this chapter is different however, here it is significant for its description of what seems very much like a second hanging bowl. Although it is not described in as much detail, it has exactly the same elements (a bowl hung on a chain over a marble slab). The only difference is that this bowl is silver rather than gold, which is a material actually occasionally used to make hanging bowls.

3. The Invisibility Ring in 'Owain'

'God knows,' said the maiden, 'it is a great shame you may not be delivered, and it would be proper for a woman to rectify that. God knows I have never seen a lad better than you for a woman. If you had a sweetheart, you would be the best admirer of a woman, and if you had a lover, you would be the best lover. And because of that' she said, 'whatever I may do to deliver you, I shall do it. Take this ring, and place [it] around your finger and place the stone inside your hand, and close your palm around the stone, and as long as you hide it, it shall hide you, for its part.'

Extract three, also from 'Owain' tells of Owain's deliverance from a strange fate. He has just poured water on the marble slab and fought with the black knight who was mentioned at the end of the last extract. He was eventually victorious in this combat, and the black knight fled from him after receiving a moral blow. Owain pursued him back to the Black Knight's town, and was just behind him. The people of the town let the portcullis fall behind the Black Knight. Owain just about made it through, but his horse was cut in half by the blow. Luned, the maiden in our story has just appeared on the other side of the portcullis, and wishes to assist Owain. Her relationship with him is purely platonic but also quite peculiar, and she ends up being a much more important character in the rest of the story that Owain's wife.

It is interesting that the ring seems to only be given to Owain because of his way with women, and that it's possible that the ring would not even have worked had Owain not been a "true knight". The ring is even taken away later on when he is unfaithful to his wife. Although Luned is seeing Owain for the first time in this scene there is the implicit belief in medieval literature (and probably medieval courtly society) that someone's looks directly reflect what sort of person they are. Thus true nobility and valour can be seen in someone's face on first meeting them. For this reason, love on first sight has slightly different connotations in medieval romances, and Luned can know that Owain would be a faithful lover just by his noble bearing and the look on his face. This topos is found very frequently in J.R.R. Tolkien's books (where certain characters can be seen to be noble or valorous on first meeting them and masterful characters can take control of another person just y looking into their eyes.)

4. The Invisibility Mantle in 'Branwen'

"Caswallon came [down] from above them and slew the six men, and from that Caradog's broke his heart from bewilderment: from seeing the sword striking the men and not knowing who struck them. Caswallon had achieved [this] for himself [by] wearing a charmed mantle around him, and no-one could see him killing the men, only the sword. Caswallon could not kill him [Caradog]: he was his nephew, son of his cousin. And he was one of the three men that broke his heart from bewilderment. Pendaren of Dyfed, who was a young man, escaped into the forest together with seven [other] men."

Extract four makes up a complete speech given to a group of people asking for the latest news of Britain. We might almost suspect that this story is only told because of what happened previously; just before this point in 'Branwen', the titular character of the story also died, and the triads list her as another of the three characters who broke their hearts from 'aniuyget' ('bewilderment' but sometimes translated 'sorrow' in context). However this revelation is actually quite relevant to the story as I said before.

Caswallon's mantle is called a 'llen hut' (mantle of charms), but 'hut a lethrith' (charms and illusion) is the normal way of expressing 'magic' in the 'Four Branches of the Mabinogi'. The idea of a sword coming out of the darkness, held by an invisible person and seeming to float inexorably towards its victim is one which has now entered the British consciousness. J.R.R. Tolkien used it quite often in his books.

5. The Invisibility Mantle in 'Rhonabwy'

And he drew the mantle before Arthur. And [there were] red-gold apples to each corner of it. And he put the chair on the mantle, and the chair was so big [that] it was able to seat three soldiers in armour. White was the name of the mantle, and one of the qualities of this mantle was [that] no-one could see the man that [was] wrapped in it, and he could see everyone. And no colour would last on it ever, except its own colour. And Arthur sat on the mantle and Owain son of Urien stood before him.

Extract five gives a mantle very similar to the one in 'Branwen' except that in this case it seems to be working with Arthur sitting above it rather than wrapped in it. However, the repeated use of this artefact demonstrates that it was a well known motif, and adds credence to the idea that it may have been an artefact "remembered" from early times rather than invented in later times.

6. The Ring of Lucidity in 'Rhonabwy'

And then Idawc said, 'Rhonabwy, do you see the ring and the stone in it on the hand of the emperor?

'Yes' he said.

'One of the powers of that gem is, you will remember what you have seen here tonight. And if you had not seen the stone, you would not remember of any of this on your waking.

Extract six gives another artefact from Rhonabwy which I mentioned earlier. For most of the story of Rhonabwy, the main character is in a dream/vision of the heroic past where he meets Arthur and some of his knights. This vision seems to have been mysteriously induced by Rhonabwy choosing to sleep on the hide of a yearling yellow heifer, but the power of this hide-skin is never explicitly acknowledged so I have not added a description of the hide-skin to this extract. However, it is interesting that it seems to take the two magic artefacts working together for Rhonabwy to both have a vision and remember it. I should also note that this ring's power is all in the stone. This seems to be the norm for magical rings in Welsh literature and is also the case with 'Owain's Ring of Invisibility which I described in extract three.

7. The Sleep-inducing Music in 'Lludd a Llefelys'

King Lludd arranged a feast to be prepared, great in amount, and after it was prepared, he brought a tub full of cold water close at hand and he personally attended to keeping watch. And while he was thus, dressed in armour, around the third watch of the night, behold he heard many rare fair tunes and various songs impelling him to sleep.

And with that, this [is] what he did, lest it hinder his intention by overcoming him, he went frequently into the water. And in the end, behold! A man, massive in size, wearing heavy, strong armour coming inside with his basket...

This account does not properly contain an artefact, but I have included it anyway because I believe it tallies well with some of the other evidence from this extract and others. As I have said before, this episode of Lludd is also found in Irish literature, but a couple of the other artefacts in this extract also have tranquilising properties. Furthermore the magician described at the end has certain similarities to the people from Annwfn, and the family of Lllwyd Cil Coed.

8. Olwen's bride-prizes in 'Culhwch ac Olwen'

a. 'The Cup of Llwyr son of Llwyrion, which will contain the head-drink. There is not a vessel in the world that can receive that strong ale except it. You won't get it from him willingly, nor will you be able to force him.'

'That's easy for me.'

b. 'Although you may get that, [what about] the Hamper of Gwyddnau Garanhir: [even] if the [whole] world came to it, every thrice-nine men [might get any] food they could want from it, according to their inclination. I would like to eat from that the night that my daughter would sleep with you. He will not give it with his permission to anyone, nor will you be able to force him.'

'That's easy for me.'

c. 'Although you may get that, [what about] the Horn of Gwlgawt of Gododdin, to serve me that night. He will not give it with his permission, nor will you be able to force him.'

'That's easy for me.'

d. 'Although you may get that, [what about] the Harp of Teirtu to entertain us that night. Whenever people may desire, it plays itself, [and] whenever it may be desired [to stop], it silences itself. He will not give it with his permission, nor will you be able to force him.'

'That's easy for me.'

e. 'Although you may get that, [what about] the Birds of Rhiannon, those that awaken the dead and send the living to sleep. I would like them to entertain me that night.'

'That's easy for me.'

f. 'Although you may get that, [what about] <u>the Cauldron of Diwrnach</u> the Gael, steward of Odgar son of Aed, lord of Ireland to boil food for your wedding.'

'That's easy for me.'

...

g. 'Although you may get that, the blood is not of benefit unless it is taken warm. There is not a vessel in the world that may keep the liquid in it warm that is put inside except <u>the Bottles of Gwyddolwyn the Dwarf</u>. They keep heat inside them [from] when the liquid is put inside them in the east until when the west is reached. He will not give it with his permission, nor will you be able to force him.'

'That's easy for me.'

h. 'Although you may get that, some will want fresh milk, it will not be possible to get milk for anyone unless <u>the Bottles of Rhinnon Rhin Barfawg</u> are got. No liquid ever sours in them. He will not give it with his permission, nor will you be able to force him.'

'That's easy for me.'

Extract eight's long extract from 'Culhwch ac Olwen' is taken from half way through the bride-price demands of Ysbaddaden Penkawr. These are the things which the father of the bride demands from the prospective groom (Culhwch) in exchange for his daughter Olwen. I have missed out a brief passage which does not contain any artefacts (marked by the ellipsis "...") but otherwise the text is continuous. In our extract Ysbaddaden demands eight powerful artefacts from Culhwch. Five of these are containers for food, two are sources of entertainment and one is the strange hamper. I will examine these in more detail in the Interpretation section.

Most of this dialogue speaks for itself but the first artefact and the one directly after the ellipsis need some explaining. The ale which is to go in the first artefact was requested just before our selection starts, and is so strong because it is to be made from exceptional honey. The artefact after the ellipsis is looking for a place to put blood because previously Ysbaddaden stated that he wished his beard to be trimmed before the wedding, and he needed special tools to help him with this (the search for these tools is the central premise of 'Culhwch').

In addition, the language used to describe the Hamper of Gwyddnau Garanhir and the Bottles of Gwyddolwyn is quite confused. The 'thrice-nine men' of the former may refer to how many typically sit in a court. In the Welsh laws as we have them there are twenty-four proper 'swyddog' (court officers). This is the normal number counted as for example described in "the Knife of Llawrfrodedd" below. If we add to them the King, Queen and Edling (Heir Apparent) this makes twenty-seven or thrice-nine, who might sit at a table together. However, according to the laws as we have them, only fourteen of these have chairs in the court[24], so perhaps this does not explain the number

---

[24] See Dafyd Jenkins, *The Law of Hywel Dda*, pp.5; 7.

properly. Likewise the journey described from the east to the west seems like it might have originally described the movement of the sun, meaning that the bottles could keep liquid warm for an entire day (12 hours), although this is not obvious from the text as we have it.

9. The "Thirteen Treasures of the Isle of Britain"

i. Dyrnwyn, the Sword of Rhydderch the Generous: if a well-born man drew it himself, it would burst into flames from its cross-[hilt] to its point, and anyone who asked for it would get it, and [yet] for the reason of that property, they would refuse it, and because of that, he was called Rhydderch the Generous.

ii. The Hamper of Gwyddno Garanhir: food for one man would be put inside it, and food for one hundred would be found inside it when it was opened.

iii. The Horn of Bran Galed: the drink that was desired to be inside would be found inside it.

iv. The Chariot of Morgan Mwynfawr: if a man went in it, he could wish to be [any] place he wished, and he would be there quickly.

v. The Halter of Clydno Eiddyn: it was inside [his] chamber below the foot of his bed, and the horse which he wished to be there, he would find.

vi. The Knife of Llawrfrodedd Farchog: this would serve twenty four men eating at a table.

vii. <u>The Cauldron of Dyrnwch Gawr:</u> if meat was for a cowardly man was put inside it to boil, it would never boil, if meat for a brave man was put inside it, it would boil quickly.

viii. <u>The Whetstone of Tudwal Tutklud:</u> A brave man could whet his sword, [then] if he drew blood from a man they would die, and if a cowardly man whetted it they would be none the worse.

ix. <u>The Tunic of Padarn Red-Tunic :</u> if a well-born man wore it, it would be to his size, but if a dishonourable man, it would not go around him.

x &xi. <u>The vat and dish of Rhygenydd the cleric:</u> The food that was desired [and] was wished inside them, he would find it.

xii. The *Gwyddbwyll*-set of Gwendolleu: if the men were set up, they would play themselves, the board was gold and the men were silver.

xiii. <u>The Mantle of Arthur:</u> whoever was under it, No-one would see him, and he would not see anyone.

xiv. <u>The Mantle of Degau Eurfron:</u> it would not serve for anyone that had broken her marriage [vows] or her maidenhood, and for anyone who was faithful to her husband, it[s hem] would be down to the ground, and for anyone that broke her marriage [vows] it would not cover as far as her lap, and because of that there was jealousy for

Degau Eurvron

xv. <u>The Stone and Ring of Eluned the Fortunate</u>, that was

given to bring Owain son of Urien who was between the

portcullis and the gate, in the competition with the Black

Knight of the fountain, this had a stone in it, and if the

stone was hidden, nothing was seen of anyone who hid it.

As I said in the introduction, this list is only attested very late on, and the last two items on the list (xiv and xv) are obviously not original to the 'Thirteen Treasures'. Nevertheless, this list does contain a some of the same artefacts which we have already seen attested earlier, and some which we do not have attested elsewhere, but are likely to be quite old. This list actually becomes a very popular text in the fifteenth century, and Welsh poets begin to quote items from it in their poems, but since these seem to be quite clearly quotations with no original material I will not give any of these late references. Intriguingly some of the manuscripts supply a subtitle "that were in the North" to our title, referring to the Welsh speaking kingdoms which occupied the border between Scotland and Wales in the first millennium A.D. Many of the characters mentioned in the list, (e.g. Rhydderch Hael) are known to have lived in the north in this time from other sources, so it is possible that some elements of this list may have some antiquity. However, given the list's fame in the fifteenth century, we can say with some certainty that the list itself did not circulate before this point.

Much of the list is characterised by items based on the medieval Welsh obsession the courtly virtuous (honour, bravery, faithfulness). In particular, vii, viii, ix and xiv serve this purpose. These are probably of limited value, although two of them: the Cauldron of Dyrnwch Gawr and The Mantle of Degau Eurfron are known in earlier texts (the latter only in French Arthurian texts). Other than these two, numbers ii (The Hamper of Gwyddno Garanhir) xiii (The Mantle of Arthur) and xv (the Stone and Ring of Eluned) we have previously seen in our extracts from this section. Number xv seems to have used our extract from 'Owain' as its only source, and therefore probably does not represent a separate tradition from our extract three But numbers ii and xiii on the other hand both give different information to that found in the previous references to them which suggests a unique lineage.

Overall the items represented in the "Thirteen Treasures" are much more varied than those we saw on the 'Culhwch' list. There is one deadly weapon (i) which should probably be grouped with the whetstone which makes any weapon deadly (viii). There is one hamper (ii) which replicates food which should probably be linked with the three items that create food (iii, x&xi). These might be linked with magic knife (vi) which together would make a feast for a court out of nothing. The horse teleporter (v) also allows immediate access to something. There are two discerning tunics which can change size (ix and xiv) and a discerning cauldron which will only boil for some (vii). Perhaps a preferred type of garment would be one of invisibility, for which we have a cloak (xiii) and a ring (xv). Unlike in the 'Culhwch' list there is only one item given purely for entertainment, the *gwyddbwyll* (a set of playing pieces for a board-game like chess) (xii). Finally there is one magical 'kar' (chariot) (iv).

10. 'Artefacts from Annwfn'

My first word, from the cauldron when it was spoken

From breath of nine maidens it was kindled

It is the Cauldron of the Head of Annwfn; what is its

nature?

A collar about the rim with pearls

It does not boil a coward's food (that has not been fated)

To it Lluch Lleawch's sword has been raised

And in the hand of Leminawc it was left

Extract ten is a small part of the text we looked at for "The Case of 'Preiddeu Annwfn'. It contains two artefacts, both said to be found in Annwfn, Lluch Lleawch's sword and the Cauldron of the Head of

Annwfn. As I said previously, the speaker at the beginning of this extract may well be supposed to be Taliesin, or a Taliesin figure. In addition, the Lluch referenced here may be a Welsh version of Lugh Lamhfada from Irish mythology, who has his own mighty sword. If this is the case, either this sword is a truly ancient relic, taken from the times before the Irish and Welsh languages split, or it represents a borrowing from Irish mythology. The latter may be more likely given the number of Irish borrowings in 'Preiddeu Annwfn'. Other than that I need only point out that the 'Head of Annwfn' seems to be an honorary chief of the Annwfn, which is of course the Celtic disappearing Otherworld we spoke about earlier, usually thought to be under the ground or across the sea (see: "The Case of Arawn of Annwfn").

11. The Cauldron of Rebirth in 'Branwen'

And then the Irish started to kindle a fire beneath The

Cauldron of Rebirth. And then corpses were thrown into

the cauldron, until they were whole [again] and they arose

the next morning, fighting men as good as before, except

they were not able to speak. And then, when Efnissyen saw

the corpses without life on the side of the men of the Isle of

the Mighty, he said in his mind:

'Alas to God,' he said 'Woe is mine that I am the cause of

this desolation of the men of the Isle of the Mighty; and

shame to me' he said 'if I do not achieve [our] deliverance

from this.'

And he hid himself among the corpses of the Irish, and two

naked Irishmen[25] came to him, and threw him into the

cauldron as one of the Irish. He stretched himself in the cauldron, until he broke the cauldron into four pieces, and then his own heart broke.

Extract eleven is another one from 'Branwen' just like extract four. The cauldron described here is a big part of 'Branwen'. It comes originally from Ireland in the hands of Llassar Llaes Gyfnewit who is a giant and a refugee (the Irish tried to kill all his kind). He escaped and gave the cauldron to Bendigeidfran, the King of Britain in return for sanctuary. Whilst in Britain he also gives his name to a special, probably blue, calquing colour and technique. Bendigeidfran then gives the cauldron as a present to Matholwch, a King of Ireland. Later on in the story, when the British come to devastate Ireland they run into trouble at this point in the narrative. All the way through Branwen the references agree that this cauldron brings anyone back to life. No matter how wounded they are. They will wake up the next day, without a scratch on them, but they will not be able to speak.

---

[25] Irish people are frequently depicted as naked in Welsh literature, most often when they fight but sometimes just in general. The origins of this are lost, but the joke has endured into the present day in the form of "What does a Scotsman wear under his kilt?" Latin reports of the continental Celtic language speaking peoples in prehistory sometimes describe them as fighting naked. It was probably perpetuated as part of a racist joke on the part of the British, but very possibly encouraged by the medieval Irish who seem to have wanted to appear "more Celtic".

Interpretation

I don't want to discuss all of the items I have listed in the texts section considering the number of them, especially in the last two texts. Some of them, for example the 'Ring of Lucidity' in 'Rhonabwy' seem to me to purely function as plot devices. Of course, just because an item is being used as a plot device does not make it less authentic, or even less interesting. One technique of becoming conscious of and later remembering dreams in modern times is to look for a detailed, familiar item, which is supposed to subtly inform the conscious mind that it is asleep, without waking it up. The ring in 'Rhonabwy', although used slightly differently still seems reminiscent of this, hence the name I have given it. Similarly, some of the items listed seem to be only slightly remarkable versions of items that were commonplace in the storyteller's world. For example artefact eight (a) from 'Culhwch' is just an exceptionally strong cup. It could have been made of something non-reactive like glass or plastic, but it could easily have just been an especially strong version of a normal cup. Likewise, for our circumstances, there is probably nothing very significant about the drinking horn described in "c" except that it belonged to Gwlgawt of Gododdin. This man is a famous steward, described in 'Y Gododdin', an old poem in which warriors feasted for a year before going to war. This is probably the medieval equivalent of Delia Smith's mixing bowl. The rest of this discussion shall be confined to those artefacts which are found in multiple sources, powers which are found on multiple artefacts, or powerful artefacts which may reflect an anachronistic technology which we can recognise.

Texts one and two refer to strikingly similar artefacts. As I said in my notes, hanging bowls are known to have been in Britain between the fourth and the seventh centuries. These are more normally copper, although silver ones have been known. Interestingly though these very similar artefacts have very different effects. The version in text two seems to almost act as a doorbell. Although the immediate effect of pouring the water on the slab seems to have been to summon a storm, the ultimate effect seems to be to bring the guardian of the fountain to fight with the trespasser. As we saw in 'Cases of Strange Sounds', storms, especially 'twrwf' occasionally mark simply the arrival or transport of the non-human entity.

The Baginton Bowl from the Herbert Art Gallery and Museum, picture taken by the Herbert Art Gallery and Museum, Coventry. Licensed for use under the "Creative Commons Attribution-Share Alike 3.0 Unported" see: http://creativecommons.org/licenses/by-sa/3.0/deed.en for more information.

The version of the hanging-bowl in text one is also interesting. The description of chains reaching up into the sky with no end makes me wonder what this hanging vessel is hanging from. Pryderi who touches it immediately becomes paralysed, and not just paralysed but comatose, with his muscles still clenched (otherwise he would fall over). This whole scene seems reminiscent of a Star Trek plot.

Nor is this stunning effect unique to text one. Twice after this, in texts seven and eight (e) we find music which sends to sleep everybody who hears it. These two texts were ones I was not sure whether I should include. In both, the source of the music is rather mysterious and not really described very well. In our extract from 'Lludd a Llefelys' only the effect is mentioned whereas in our extract from 'Culhwch' the text describes birds as the source. Of course, it is possible that these texts do record modern technology. The concept of recorded music may have been quite difficult to grasp for a medieval audience, and perhaps the easiest way to describe this music would be that it was like an instrument which played itself, an explanation which actually was used to describe the Harp of Teritu (eight d).

Hypnotising, soporific, hard-to-resist music is still a popular idea in our own time, but scientists have yet to invent it. However, the use of sonic weapons is now fairly common. Even in the Second World War, the Axis reputedly developed a Sonic Canon able to resonate with tissues in vital organs. The recent "SpeechJammer" gun created by Kazutaka Kurihara and Koji Tsukada prevents and cuts-off people from speaking by firing a certain type of sound which creates a feedback effect in human brains. Similarly, the controversial LRAD sonic weapon and hailing device has been deployed successfully at various riots and against pirates. In current times it is being used by the UK police force to help police the London Olympic Games of 2012. The LRAD can be used as a loudspeaker, but can also serve as a non-lethal weapon by creating a very loud sound. This can cause pain, nausea, vomiting and even permanent ear damage, especially on high settings or at close range. The use of non-fatal sonic weapons has truly begun in earnest over the last ten years, and it may not be long before we are able to replicate the music described in these stories.

The LRAD (speaker is the round device at the top left of the picture) here mounted on a U.S. Navy vessel. Image by Lradcorporation, licensed under the GNU v1.2. See:
https://commons.wikimedia.org/wiki/Commons:GNU_Free_Documentation_License_1.2?uselang=en-gb
For more details.

However our collection of artefacts is not confined to non-violent ones. The Sword of Lluch Lleawch and Dyrnwyn, the Sword of Rhydderch the Generous both seem to describe lightning swords. The name of the former can be rendered the sword of 'lightning's slaughter'[26], whereas the latter is described as fiery. 'Lluch' (lightning) may actually be an

---

[26] Koch and Carey, *The Celtic Heroic Age*, p.310.

alternate form of 'Llacher' (radiant). This is a fairly common name, and an incredibly common description used to describe swords and spears in 'Y Gododdin' and other early poetry. There is also a fragment of poetry in 'Kat Godeu', a poem ascribed to Taliesin which may describe a related figure:

> My blood-spattered sword
>
> Brings me to honourable bloodshed
>
> From the Lord, from the burial place where he was
>
> By a meek one the boar was slain
>
> He made, he unmade
>
> He made peoples
>
> Llachar [was] his name, (strong-handed one)
>
> Lluch directed a host
>
> They scattered in sparks
>
> From a drop in the heights

This extract clearly breaks into two parts. The first six lines end in –d (a "th" sound) whereas the last four lines end in -r. The first part of this verse is very uncertain and may be completely unrelated to the second part[27]. However the second part seems clearer to me. 'Llawfer' (strong-handed), seems very similar to Lamhfada (long handed), the name used to describe Lugh in Irish mythology. Our original name 'Lluch' comes in the very next line suggesting it may be a variant name. In addition the meaning of the passage is quite clear: Llachar (radiant one) who is called Lluch (bright) scattered sparks by dropping from the heights (a lightning bolt). I have said that this part of the poem may describe a god, and this is one of the only cases in medieval Welsh literature (a highly Christian medium) where anything like a pagan god is described, but the

---

[27] See Marged Haycock's notes in *Legendary Poems from the Book of Taliesin* (pp.231-2). She suggests the first part may be referring to God, and Jesus' resurrection.

character here may well be a lightning god. The Norse, Latin, Greek and Sanskrit all have gods of heaven possessed of a lightning bolt which they use to attack others with. In Sanskrit the thing is called the 'vajra' although this word is also used more generically for other similarly-shaped tools. As we have seen, aliens in medieval British literature may have been quite capable of creating storms (See: "Cases of Strange Sounds"). Could these fiery swords and perhaps even the weapons of the various gods of thunder found throughout the world preserve memories of contact with species who actually have the technology to launch lightning bolts and bring storms?

The Jupiter of Smyrna, a mid-second century statue of Jupiter complete with a thunderbolt in his right hand. Picture taken by Marie-Lan Nguyen, 2009 and released into the public domain.

Moving on, the most common type of artefact described in our extracts is an invisibility mantle. They are variously described in texts four, five, and nine (xiii). The mantles in texts five and nine both belonged to [King] Arthur, which may suggest a common source. Alternatively, it is possible that the description in 'The Thirteen Treasures of the Isle of Britain' is derivative of the one in 'Rhonabwy'. This seems less likely to me, considering that 'Rhonabwy' has some details that 'The Thirteen Treasures' does not, and also how much detail text nine (xv) gives about

Owain's ring but it is certainly possible. The mantle in 'Branwen' however does not share any link with the other texts. Neither Arthur nor any of his other artefacts appear in 'the Mabinogi', and these texts could have been written before Arthur became popular.

The invisibility cloak is another item which humans are on the cusp of developing. The nearest prototype currently in existence may be the creation of Professor Susumu Tachi at Keio University.[28] The idea of "retro-reflective projection technology" is simply to project an image on one side of a body of the view from the other side of it (and vice versa if invisibility rather than one-way transparency is desired). So far the technology is only claimed to be "optical camouflage" rather than true invisibility, and would only completely conceal someone who is staying still and who is at some distance from the viewer (it works best in two dimensional flat surfaces rather than human bodies). Currently it also requires a separate (visible) camera and projector, making the person quite obvious. On the other hand, the cloak prototype was given worldwide coverage in the media in 2009, and Tachi Laboratory seems optimistic about market uses ("invisible" car-fenders and plane cockpits). Other methods of invisibility being investigated by teams in Britain and America involve diverting light around objects with none of it reflecting (the technique used to "cloak" aircraft) and various "mirage" effects. Finally it is worth pointing out that there are rumours (and various dubious video evidences) that the technology has already been perfected by the US military.

Interestingly, even though Medieval Welsh does not even have a word for 'invisible' (see my translations above for how the concept was expressed), the extracts we have seen are fairly accurate portrayals of the technology we have. Every single method of making somebody invisible which I have seen requires that person to be entirely wrapped in the cloak, which is exactly the method of wearing it which is emphasised in our sources. Even in 'Rhonabwy', where Arthur is sitting on a chair over the cloak, the text emphasises he needed to be wrapped in it to be invisible. Although it is conceivable that a cloak wrapped tight (with a low hood/mask) could be nearly completely invisible, a sword in

---

[28] See: (http://www.youtube.com/watch?v=PD83dqSfC0Y) and (http://www.youtube.com/watch?v=gSZcbfu3pK8).

somebody's hand would be fully visible, which is exactly what is described in 'Branwen'.

Considering this fairly realistic portrayal of the currently achievable (or nearly achievable) invisibility cloak, it is quite interesting that an invisibility ring seems very nearly as popular as an invisibility mantle. These are seen in 'Owain' and also again in the 'Thirteen Treasures' text. As I noted earlier however, the ring is probably not original to the 'Thirteen Treasures', especially considering that it is the fifteenth of them! In addition, the description of the ring in this text paraphrases 'Owain', and has exactly the same description of the ring as in 'Owain'. This strongly suggests that it is just a late reference back to 'Owain' and not an independent source. Given that 'Owain' is most likely a thirteenth or fourteenth century text, it is quite conceivable that the motif of a ring of invisibility was merely a late variation of the motif of the mantle with no basis in reality or history whatsoever.

The Hamper of Gwyddnau Garanhir is also an intriguing artefact. There are two descriptions of it in my extracts, you can find it in eight (b) and also nine (ii). These two descriptions have important differences. In the 'Culhwch' extract, it will produce food for the whole world, according to what every thrice-nine want to eat, and in the 'Thirteen Treasures' extract it will replicate food enough for one-hundred men. These descriptions are perfect in variety. They are similar enough so that we can see that the hamper was originally something which kept producing food even for huge numbers of people, but different enough so that they probably reflect varying traditions about it.

The description in the 'Thirteen Treasures' is especially interesting, because it represents a method of creation which was found very commonly in our own science-fiction fifty years ago. The idea was that anything could be put into a machine, and its exact chemical pattern would be studied, and then "cloned" in the other side of the machine. This concept formed the basis for many nineteenth and twentieth century stage magicians' big finales, but seems to have lost its popularity recently, perhaps with the invention of genetic cloning. Nevertheless, the idea is still found in Star Trek's transporters, and, more closely, in the "replicators" which produce food and drink on command according to a series of chemical template patterns in the ship's computer. However, as far as I am aware this technology still as out of reach for us as it was for the nineteenth century magicians and fifteenth century author of 'The Thirteen Treasures'. The closest we are able to come is with 3D printing. The "Choc Creator Version 1" by Choc Edge, first shipped in April 2012 allows users to "print out" any size, shape and colour of chocolate with a special printer using a 3D pattern sent to the printer by computer. However this printer currently still requires chocolate material as an input and therefore is nowhere near as efficient and useful as a "cloning" device which would clone the matter out of pure energy (and be able to create any food)

The description of the Hamper of Gwyddnau Garanhir in 'Culhwch' is also interesting as it closely resembles a number of the other artefacts which create whatever food is desired in 'The Thirteen Treasures', such as iii, and x &xi which even use similar language. These are most likely to have been based on descriptions of the hamper. Since none of these mention requiring an example before additional meals are created, perhaps that element of the description in "The Thirteen Treasures" was a late interpolation. On the other hand, other food creation stories, like for example Jesus' two food miracles in the gospels[29], do typically also require an "exemplar" food source in order to clone additional food, so the 'Thirteen Treasures' version may even be the original.

The last artefact which is repeated multiple times is 'The Cauldron of Dyrnwch Gawr'. This is found in 8 (f) 9 (vii) and 10. In our extract from 'Culhwch' the cauldron is not described as having any special powers, and seems to be just a cauldron. On the contrary, in our extract from 'The Thirteen Treasures' this cauldron is very clearly said to have the property of only boiling the food of the brave. The names of these two artefacts have only a minor variation in spelling (attributable to irregular orthography and the between three and six hundred years which separate the writing of the two accounts), and it is clear that they are talking about the same artefact. This might lead us to believe that the story was invented later on after the time of Culhwch when no story was given for the cauldron. However this does not seem to be the case. 'Preiddeu Annwfn' which may even predate 'Culhwch' also records this story that the cauldron will not boil a cowards food, although that poem

---

[29] A miracle of five loaves and two fishes is found in Matthew (14:17-20), Mark (8: 38-44), Luke (9:13-17) and John (6: 10-13), but a miracle of seven loaves and some fish is also found in Matthew (15:33-38).

does has a different name for the cauldron. It is conceivable that there might originally have been two cauldrons, one with the name of 'Dyrnwch' attached to it, and the other with the properties of only serving brave men. This idea is given some support by the fact not all manuscript versions of 'Preiddeu Annwfn' name Dyrnwch – some just name it 'The Cauldron'.

Sadly this kind of discerning artefact seems to me the least likely of all of our artefacts to be referencing any real historic artefact. The technology is nothing too impressive. We have biometric scanners, password protected computer assisted machinery and many other ways to allow only a machine to only work for a select group of people. This sort of thing may well have been explained in terms of some personal merit possessed by the in-group, and the story could have spread from there. However, I just don't think it's realistic to say that this is due to technology rather than born from the class-obsessed medieval Welsh mind. The same objection goes for the other discerning artefacts, including the often quoted Mantle of Degau Eurfron.

Another important cauldron is the so called 'cauldron of rebirth' (y peir dadeni). Although this cauldron is only really mentioned in 'Branwen' among medieval texts, it has been seized in the popular imagination as the quintessential "Celtic" myth. If this was all there was to recommend the artefact we might safely ignore it. However, there is another possible reference to the myth in pre-medieval "Celtic" artwork which you can see below:

Gundestrupp Cauldron Interior plate E. The large figure on the left apears to be thrusting a man into a cauldron.
Photograph by Malene Thyssen. (http://commons.wikimedia.org/wiki/User:Malene) shared under a creative commons license.

This cauldron is famous for possibly depicting the prehistoric Celtic horned god "Cernunnos" (on another plate) but in some ways this plate is more interesting. What is the large figure supposed to be doing? Is the large figure cooking a human to eat them, as our own folkloric giants do, or could they be resurrecting them? The cauldron is interestingly far smaller than the one described in Branwen. If the cauldron is drawn to scale with the horsemen, warriors, standard bearers and dog rather than with the giant it seems just like an ordinarily sized cooking vessel.

If we accept an eleventh century date for Branwen, then this picture was likely created one thousand years earlier and (most likely) in a different country (fifty human generations). On the other hand, this need not necessarily be a problem. The scenes on this cauldron could easily be made into medieval Welsh style legends, and we saw in the introduction some examples of thousand year survivals of culture.

Could the cauldron of rebirth be an account of an alien technology? Although human technology is very far from being able to awaken the dead, we do not have to turn to science fiction to find accounts of it. Haitian accounts of Bokar priests, able to create "zombies" using various powerful drugs which render humans comatose have been popularised in US culture. Indeed, more than one quiet news week in 2012 was filled with accounts of an approaching zombie apocalypse, fuelled by stories of diseased humans allegedly found attempting to eat other humans alive. The truth of the matter is perhaps best discussed in *The Serpent and the Rainbow* by Dr. Wade Davis which popularly systematised the various drugs used to place people into comas from which they can awake with no will of their own. With this in mind it is quite conceivable that our account of people waking up without the power of speech is a reflection of some prehistoric experimentation with such drugs. However there is not nearly enough evidence to suggest that this is anything other than a fictional motif, and certainly not enough evidence to implicate an alien race.

Having covered all of the repeating items, I would like to discuss three more artefacts before ending the chapter. Although these items are not repeated, they so closely resemble modern-day technology that I felt it important to mention them. The first of these is the Chariot of Morgan

Mwynfawr in extract nine (iv). This artefact is incredibly exciting because it is the only reference I am aware of to a chariot in medieval Welsh literature, although chariots are incredibly common in early Irish literature. Although Caesar attests to the use of war chariots in Britain when he invaded, and we know chariot racing was common in Roman Britain they are not found in the vernacular literature, and must have fell out of use before the medieval period. We do not even frequently see carts or wagons, which might be explained as reflecting the aristocratic bias of Medieval Welsh texts. This chariot is made even more exciting by its description. In the context of 'The Thirteen Treasures' we should probably understand the description to mean that a person need only wish to be somewhere, and they would be taken there very quickly, without having to do any work. Interestingly the English language already coined a word for a device like this. Something that works by itself is called auto-, and a device that moves is called mobile, so we find that the English word "automobile" in its original sense exactly described this device. Although you may not feel like your car drives itself, since it is not pulled by horses or oxen, and since it does not need you to push it (normally), from a medieval point of view it would have been considered a marvel.

In the last chapter on "Cases of Strange Sounds" I hypothesised that a 'twrwf' may have originally been the sound of a non-human entity arriving very fast in a vehicle, and breaking the sound barrier. I even gave a picture of a human version of this technology at the end of the chapter. Could this artefact be one of those vehicles? Could it be a British version of the legendary Sanskrit vimānas popularised Erich Däniken? The possibility is there, but the text does not describe the chariot flying, merely being fast and self-propelled. We do definitely have here a marvellous artefact easily explainable by modern technology, but quite which modern technology is more difficult to decide.

Finally, I would like to turn my attention to two more artefacts. These are both bottles in 'Culhwch', extract 8 (g &h). To begin with the Bottles of Gwyddolwyn the Dwarf, these were said to keep any liquid hot from the east to the west. As I said before, the east to west probably refers to the movement of the sun, so we are considering bottles which will work for an average of twelve hours (according to British day lengths). This medieval marvel would not be very difficult for a modern Culhwch to get hold of – the average Thermos flask off the shop shelf in modern times will keep liquid hot for only eight hours, but some will work for up to 24 hours with minimal heat loss. The technology of the Thermos, or vacuum flask as it was originally called, is quite simple. There are two bottles, one entirely inside the other. In the centre the air between the bottles is removed, meaning that heat cannot transfer out of the bottle (convection and conduction of heat are impossible in a vacuum, only radiation is possible).

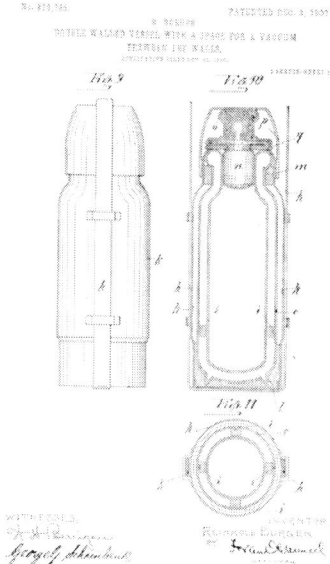

The original 1907 patent.

In our example, the substance being transported in the bottle is very interesting. That substance is blood, and the text stresses that it needs to be kept hot. This is interesting because in modern times human blood is, of course, very often transported for infusions. However blood is normally moved at low temperatures of 2-10° C rather than at warm temperatures. This is to stop the breakdown of the live components. Presumably blood might be kept warm if there was no way to chill it, and warm it up, or if another method was found to stop it breaking down (perhaps the admission of a chemical preservative?) or if the blood was going to be used immediately. Then again, in these texts we are looking for old motifs not old stories. If these bottles were well known artefacts, perhaps they were only known to maintain the heat of liquids, and transporting blood in them was first advocated in 'Culhwch', in which case we need not wonder that the blood was transported hot and not cold. This is suggested by the wording. The word 'blood' is only used before the bottles are introduced. The bottles themselves however are only said to be able to transfer 'llyn' ('a liquid' here but more normally 'a drink', 'an alcoholic beverage') without losing temperature. This suggests they were not normally used for blood. In any case, here is another marvellous artefact we have since invented.

Likewise, the Bottles of Rhinnon Rhin Barfawg, which stop any liquid (milk in this instance) from ever souring within it. If we allow this to be a poetic exaggeration a modern day fridge would easily serve this function. Before the advent of pasteurisation, milk left in a cellar or shed to stay cool would only last a day (depending on temperature), but "raw milk" will last in a fridge for at least a week. To my knowledge scientists have yet to invent a standalone refrigerated bottle (perhaps because small portable coolers are very common, and already chilled items can be kept cool in thermos flasks). On the other hand, the technology could probably be created without too much trouble, so this could easily be another example of modern technology.

Of course, if some of the artefacts in this section do represent alien technology, the question remains, where are they now? Archaeological excavations and relics in churches and palaces and mansions all tend to paint a cohesive picture of the technology available to medieval people, and thermos flasks and automobiles are definitely not on this list, that is why they have since been "invented" in modern times. Although artefacts with securely-datable anachronistic levels of technology are occasionally found[30], I do not know of any in Britain which cannot be explained by contamination of the archaeological record.

One potential explanation for this problem is that most of the artefacts we have discussed in this section are unique, meaning that there was only ever one of them in the world. Considering this it is quite possible that we just have not found some of these items yet. Only a fraction of

---

[30] Two of the best accepted examples of these include the Antikythera mechanism, which is a clockwork astrological device, akin to our analogue computers created in the 1st century BC, and the Baghdad Batteries which were creations of the early first millennium A.D. and able to produce electricity.

the medieval archaeological sites in Britain have been "excavated". Most excavations are commercial which means that the focus is on the archaeology which will be destroyed. Only the area which is about to be dug up by construction workers will be even looked at by archaeologists. This means that if a house is to be built for example, archaeologists may be justified in excavating as far as the bottom of the foundations but no further. Even in the rarer research archaeology, carried out by universities, rich researchers and philanthropic organisations, excavation usually only includes a few ditches, pits and geophysical surveys. This is fairly successful at interpreting the purpose of sites and drawing an overall map but artefacts can easily escape notice.

The problem of "where are they now?" was also apparently felt in the late medieval period as one very late text from around 1566, quoted by Rachel Bromwich in her edition of the story (*Trioedd Ynys Prydein*, p.261), gives an explanation:

> The Horn of Bran Galed was one of the Thirteen Lordly Treasures of the Island of Britain. And Myrddin came there to ask the treasures from everyone wherever they were. And everyone agreed that if he got the Horn of Bran Galed he would get theirs from them, under the impression that he would not get the horn at all. But for [all] that, Myrddin got the Horn and after that he got the whole [set], and he went with them to the glass house and they [shall remain] there forever more.

The name 'ty gwydr' (glass house) is clearly supposed to be a version of the 'Glass Fort' and 'tower of glass' which we saw were entrances to Annwfn in "The Case of 'Preiddeu Annwfn'". The story therefore suggests two things, first that all of the thirteen treasures may have been from Annwfn, and secondly that they were taken back to Annwfn, thus explaining why they can no longer be found. Could this reflect an old explanation? I am not so sure. This story is only in one late manuscript, which is not a good reflection on its authenticity. The language is approximately the same age as the story of the Thirteen Treasures, (fifteen or sixteenth century) which also does not stir confidence. I would therefore suggest that it is only a late story invented to explain the absence of any of these artefacts in sixteenth century Britain. Even if our powerful artefacts are reflections of real pieces of technology, it seems unlikely that any alien race would be too dismayed by the disappearance of a few examples, even if humanity managed to acquire a replicator or automobile. If these items ever did have a real existence, some of them are probably still around, buried in ruins, buried with great princes or just waiting to be found in the attics and wardrobes of old houses and churches[31].

To sum up, this chapter has scoured the earliest literature and came up with a long list of artefacts in literature which may represent the memory of pieces of advanced technology. We have seen various paralysing artefacts, a hamper which replicates food, an invisibility cloak, an automobile and two temperature controlled flasks. But there is no conclusive evidence here. It is just as possible that humanity has been most motivated to create technology which answers its oldest dreams (flight, invisibility etc.). Although the possibility exists that these marvels, especially those repeated and obviously known at an early period, may reflect the amazing technology of a group of space travellers, it is equally possible that these marvels represent human imagination, which has always preceded human endeavour. The ultimate fact of the matter is that only very few of these artefacts have yet to be created by our current technology, but quite what this means is probably a question best left to the reader's discretion.

---

[31] One of the most important Medieval British manuscripts, The Hendregadredd Manuscript, dating to the late thirteenth or early fourteenth century, was found in the bottom of a wardrobe in the Hendregadredd mansion in Wales in 1910.

Conclusions

Piecing together the evidence

In our investigation of the history and legends of Celtic Britain we have found at least three distinct races of non-human visitors to Britain. The most commonly mentioned of these are the people from Annwfn. They inhabit an underground world, which is described as across the sea in a couple of early legends, just like the Otherworld in Irish mythology.

Since Annwfn was the "stock" Otherworld, it tends to have a gravitational effect on other peoples and magical artefacts so that everything strange is thought to belong there. However, amongst the various stock material and the later embellishments there is some material which is either frequently repeated or just seems older and more genuine. Annwfn in later mythology seems to be accessible anywhere, especially if one has a leucistic (white) creature as a guide. However, there is a repeated motif of a floating tower of glass which seems to form a portal to the underworld (See especially "The Case of 'Preiddeu Annwfn'"). This tower seems to be able to submerge itself, leading to my suggestion that it may function as a submarine. Annwfn seems to belong by Dyfed in the later legends, possibly under the Irish Sea or the Atlantic Ocean, although it may well stretch much further than this, since any deep hole in the ground was thought to go to Annwfn.

Annwfn seems to be the location in which many artefacts belong, most especially the Cauldron of Diwrnach but also many other artefacts (more on this later). It is ruled over by a king, the best known of which seems to be King Arawn, and the name 'Pen Annwfn' (Head of Annwfn) may have been the ruler's official title. However there is a discrepancy in the reaction of the people of Annwfn to humans. In most of the later prose narratives they seem friendly, and are very culturally compatible with the Britons to the extent that they are depicted as almost entirely human. They are closely associated with leucistic animals, and may have brought new breeds of pigs, deer and cattle to Britain. However, in the Glass Tower legends they seem to be quite callous, unwilling or unable to speak to humans and ruthlessly causing their death by waiting for them all to be standing by the tower and then submerging it.

The second most popularly depicted race of non-human visitors to Britain in medieval times are a race without a clear name. They are variously called the 'Eingl' (angels) and 'gwyrda' (gentlemen) in "The Case of 'Marwnad Ithel ap Robert". However they are distinguishable by their technology. They come from the sky, and they do not seem to interact with humans nearly as often as the people of Annwfn. Their ships bring natural disasters in their wake which is reminiscent of the callousness in the early accounts of the people of Annwfn. Perhaps their depiction as 'gentlemen' and fellow mourners in 'Marwnad Ithel ap Robert' is attributable to the influence of the people from Annwfn, rather than to their memory.

I said this race is quite popularly depicted because the strange lights in the sky in "Cases of UFOs in the 'Anglo Saxon Chronicle' may also depict this race. As I said in that chapter, there is a motif of describing UFOs along with disease, earthquakes and famine to provide a dramatic backdrop to hard events, like when the Vikings raided Lindisfarne. However, in my opinion this dramatic motif was probably conceived by observation of UFOs which really did bring natural disasters in their wake. The similarities between these UFOs and the Eingl as depicted in "The Case of 'Marwnad Ithel ap Robert'" are marked, if not certain. However, if these two accounts do depict the same race, then the 'Eingl' may well be the most recent group of non-human visitors to Britain in medieval literature, since their arrival actually seems to have been recorded fist hand.

The UFOs in the 'Anglo Saxon Chronicle' have various forms, the most notable of which was probably the dragon-star, which is a creation like a comet with long lasers coming out of it, and with the shape of a dragon in the front. The significance of this shape is now probably lost but it remains one of the earliest attested UFOs in Britain. Another common form of UFO is the sometimes fiery 'wolcen', which presumably resembles a cloud. This UFO appears to have acquired its own name, so may well have been very common indeed.

The final species we have seen is the Coranieid, a race which is defined by being able to hear everything. As I said in "The Case of the Coranieid", this attribute can be explained simply by extensive use of electronic bugging equipment and concealed surveillance equipment.

Unfortunately this race is, to my knowledge, only found in one story, so is the most likely of all of them to be fictional.

These races have various similarities and differences with each other. For example, the 'Eingl' and the people of 'Annwfn' both seem to be (at face value) friendly to humans, at least when they are in Britain, whereas the Coranieid were a terrible oppression on the island. However, all three of the races are able to disguise themselves and appear to be exactly like humans. This ability is very interesting. I said earlier that the ability to change form is also common to certain humans, and this suggests that the ability may not reflect a real memory of alien species. On the other hand, it is at least possible that it may reflect a historic truth about visitors. The fact that this characteristic is shared by all of the races is also interesting in that it suggests that there might be something about humans which makes them easy to fool. There is a theory on the fringe of alien-contact theory that suggests that all humans have a psychic switch hardwired into their brain that allows any race of alien with psychic ability to appear completely disguised to them whenever they choose[32]. If this theory were true it might explain the ease with which most of the non-human species in Britain seem to resemble humans. However, a psychic suggestion is clearly not the basis of the disguise by the time the latest legends were written. If, for example, everyone in Annwfn appeared human to humans, but normally to each other, Pwyll could certainly not have disguised himself among them. However the original aliens (if there were any) who inspired the stories may well have used a psychic disguise. In that case the idea of them physically changing into humans could just reflect the human perspective of them.

On the other hand, it would not require too much coincidence for three races to share that characteristic, which is very common for "Otherworldly" characters in Celtic literature. Another common motif, shared by the Coranieid and the people of Annwfn is the "kryptonite effect" which I discussed earlier. Both of these races, despite physically resembling humans are more susceptible to certain things than humans.

---

[32] This theory is probably most prevalent among those who believe in the Reptilian conspiracy, possibly due to the influence of the Lacerta files (see: http://www.luisprada.com/Protected/the_lacerta_files.htm) which calls it a switch placed in the human mind by the Illojim (Elohim).

The Coranieid could be killed by contact with bugs crushed in water, whereas this mixture did not hurt any humans. Pwyll was able to kill Hafgan of Annwfn with one blow, as long as he did not strike more than once. This does not only demonstrate that the races are physiologically different, despite their disguises, but also that they are not invulnerable and that their physical bodies are important to them. In the "Case of the Coranieid" this also demonstrated that they were hegemonic, that is, that they are all of the same race with the same weakness. However, not all of the inhabitants of Annwfn can be killed with a single blow. This might mean that they are not hegemonic to the same degree, but alternatively it might simply be an indication of how many stories of strange beings the name Annwfn has attracted to itself.

We also have some indication of the technology of these races. The "Cases of Strange Sounds" do not really neatly fit any single one of the races, which might suggest that more than one of them possessed the technology to travel faster than the speed of sound. We know that one of their vessels at least may have travelled on the ground since we saw the auto-mobile chariot in "Cases of Powerful Artefacts". There we also saw that the people of Annwfn may have possessed a weapon (ostensibly a sword) with the ability to call down lightning (which may also have inspired the other literatures of the world). Also, many of the UFOs described in the 'Anglo Saxon Chronicle' had lasers and beams of light attached. The Eingl of course brought storms and earthquakes in their wake, although it's hard to see how much control they had over these. Within the "Cases of UFOs in the 'Anglo Saxon Chronicle'" however, one of the annals is worth repeating. The annal of 1122 described a fire which waxed up against a 'wolcen', and the 'wolcen' tried to extinguish it. This might suggest a battle between two groups of alien. Now, we know the people of Annwfn are associated with surface dwelling, and especially the sea (where the fire was) and the Eingl may be associated with the air and with 'wolcnes' (that's the plural of 'wolcen') like in the other stories of UFOs. Therefore, it could be that the fire described here is a weapon of Annwfn against the Eingl. It is significant that the Eingl were unable to extinguish the fire, which may suggest that the weapons of Annwfn are more powerful.

If we were to take all three of the races as based in truth, the story would emerge of a long history of alien contact in Britain. The people of Annwfn arrived first, and they settled underground and under the sea, probably more because they wanted to be left alone than out of any respect for the powers of the Britons. Nevertheless, they did seem to occasionally mix with the people of Britain, and some of their technology was disseminated to their fortunate friends. Next in line would come the Coranieid. They did not attempt any invasion by force, but inseminated themselves into British culture with their technology, perhaps to take over and garner slaves. Presumably either the people of Annwfn did not care about this, or they were unable to do anything (perhaps they were unable to distinguish the Coranieid from humans as well). Last the Eingl would come. After sparring with the people of Annwfn a few times, they must have realised they could not overcome them, and were perhaps not permitted to live in Britain. However, the people of Annwfn were either unable, or not motivated to completely forbid them from the planet Earth and so they did occasionally visit, notably on the year of the funeral of Ithel ap Robert, but also at other times. In fact their craft were well known enough to become a common motif in the Anglo Saxon Chronicle and were called 'wolcnes'. Perhaps they had a peaceful relationship at times.

Evaluation

> But I who wrote this 'history' or rather, fable do not have
> faith in certain things [of] the history or 'fable'. Certain
> things there truly are the illusions of demons, certain other
> things are figments of poetry, certain things are similar to
> the truth, certain things are not, [and] certain things are for
> the delight of idiots.
>
> (Colophon to the 'Táin Bó Cúailnge', the greatest Old Irish
> epic, preserved in a twelfth century manuscript)

If we are seeking the truth, this piecing together of the history of contact in Britain is hard to justify. Despite all of our evidence, it is very unlikely that all of these races actually existed let alone coexisted. Although 'Annwfn' is occasionally referred to outside of fairytale, and the whole Anglo-Saxon chronicle, including the appearance of the UFOs, is supposed to be non-fiction, the Coranieid at least are only attested in one story, and therefore are most likely fictional.

In fact, if we look critically at our conclusions, very few of them stand up under scrutiny as probable truths. All we really have are a series of unexplained phenomena, and a superstitious belief in non-human races inhabiting a world just out of reach. It is certainly significant that other than a few minor features there are no technologically intelligent, organised, non-human races in Old English history and legend. There are hero-figures like Wayland and villains like Grendel and various early references to the ælfes and their ælf-shot which is what causes nightmares and cattle to sicken, but ultimately the non-human races in Old English literature are unconvincing for a race of aliens[33]. However 'The Peterborough Chronicle' has a fully developed genre of UFO

---

[33] If general Norse Folklore was used to augment the Anglo Saxon stock, a better argument might be able to be made.

sightings, and many of the sightings made there are incredibly compelling, even by modern standards.

Medieval Welsh has the opposite problem. There are almost no stories of UFOs or craft at all. There is only the one reference to an automatic chariot, and the strange lights in "The Case of 'Marwnad Ithel ap Robert'". The story of the dragon-star may possibly have been Welsh in origin, but it is now unattested in Welsh literature, suggesting that it was not a popular topos. However, there are many legends in Welsh history and legend of other races, and these quite convincingly describe intelligent, technologically proficient aliens.

The fact that each genre only exists in one literature is suggestive of the extent to which a language's genres shape which stories survive. It seems probable that the Welsh should have observed some unexplained phenomena in the sky, but no substantial body of sightings survive. This further suggests that we might not be able to trust what has survived, since it could easily be just the latest fantasy in a long line of fantasies. Perhaps the only truly trustworthy records are those which are completely unexpected and would have been very hard to make up. "The Case of 'Marwnad Ithel ap Robert'" for example, seems to tell a completely new story, and not draw on previous motifs very much at all.

On the other hand, it certainly is true that those who are interested in something do the best job recording it. For example, a medieval astrologer could certainly give a better answer about strange night-time sky phenomena than a prince, but a prince could probably answer better about politics and current affairs. If we asked them both about phenomena in the night sky over the last year, we might believe that the astrologer was making many of the things up, since the merchant could corroborate only a fraction of the things that the astrologer could name. But in reality, the astrologer's answer would be much more reliable because an astrologer is a trained, first hand observer who has devoted more time to the question. Perhaps we should simply view the Old English authors as a group of astrologers, and the medieval Welsh authors as a group of aristocrats.

Ultimately, the Celtic History and Legends we have been reading from Britain do provide documentary evidence for aliens in medieval Britain. However, evidence should not be confused with proof. Just like in the quote from the 'Táin' above, some of our "evidence" is utterly fictional while some of it is fictional with a kernel of truth. Likewise, some of it is utterly factual while some of it has only a thin veneer of fact. None of the evidence I gave here will convince anyone that aliens have definitely visited the earth, but I hope that my readers will agree that a rational person can interpret the evidence in that way.

My job in this book is really only to provide the medieval British evidence for aliens without mistranslating or misinterpreting the texts, and without misleading my readers. At the least, I hope I have convinced you of my two starting boasts: (i) There was a general belief in medieval Britain that non-human people had visited in the past and may still be around, and (ii) that certain strange events, descriptions and artefacts described in British history and legends can be interpreted as memories of anachronistic technology. Whether these findings suggest that the non-human peoples in medieval history and legends were actually an alien species, or whether the findings should be seen as purely coincidental I leave up to my readers.

####

If you enjoyed this book or have any questions or comments I would love to hear from you. My email address is:
(melissa.westwind@gmail.com).

CPSIA information can be obtained at www.ICGtesting.com
Printed in the USA
LVOW07s2104220914

405275LV00026B/1125/P